@home in Dubai

GETTING CONNECTED ONLINE AND ON THE GROUND

First Published Great Britain 2011

by Summertime Publishing

ISBN: 978-1-904881-5-99

Book Design by Creationbooth www.creationbooth.com

Dedication

This book is dedicated to M.T. who always knew I'd be an author (or a children's show host). Thanks for all your loving support from the day I was born through all my international gadding about.

@Home in Dubai...
Getting Connected Online and on the Ground

Table of Contents

Foreword   1

Introduction 5

Foreword

When epic events in life take place, you do not realize their significance, unless you can look back and mull over the lessons they taught you.

When I arrived in Dubai 12 years ago, on my husband Pawan's visa with two toddlers in tow, settling down was easy. I did not have to stand in immigration queues... it was all arranged very graciously as a corporate service to the new employee. House hunting was ruled out as we arrived a year later than him and he had found out the best place for our family, a home where my children enjoyed growing up.

However, a couple of years later our idyllic reverie was rudely interrupted when Pawan changed jobs and had to be posted out of Dubai. This was not a smooth transition and was fraught with several hiccups.

This time there was no help and I struggled to understand the immigration laws, stood in queues at the Dubai Naturalization and Residency Department (DNRD) to get my sponsorship changed, sponsor my children and worse still, sponsor my husband for his visits to the UAE.

I grew up overnight, learning all the ins and outs of the law by default. Since I had no help, I would just camp at the DNRD every morning with my papers, requesting to see the head. I must have spent hours and days at the DNRD where my face became so familiar that people just got friendly because they felt I was someone they had to see everyday. Eventually, I was able to get my work done. It was trial by fire for me, one that I am not likely to forget easily.

I wish I had a book like Anne O'Connell's @*Home in Dubai...Getting Connected Online and on the Ground* then; a book that could have been my comfort in a friendless city.

Settling down in a new country can be a nightmare, and a book like this can help demystify the intricacies of official and social life. Written in the most conversational, witty and concise manner, Anne's book is like the much-needed hospitable host, who agrees to hold your hand through the raw and rough days of migrating to a new country.

Like a ready reckoner, it has everything that you would need while moving to the UAE. In other words, the book gives you a 360 view of what life in Dubai entails and how to take the rough in with the smooth.

It is just the kind of book you are going to love as it organises your thoughts on the topic breaking down complicated information into bite-sized pieces that are easy to digest. It's a book that is bound to be every greenhorn's almanac to Dubai.

In many ways, the book is what Anne stands for—the warmest friend in need. When I met her a few years ago as the outgoing head of the Dubai Chapter of Room to

Read, a charity that looks to provide libraries and reading facilities for schools in impoverished regions of the world, she was already glowing with this positive energy that she had derived from her work.

We had an instant rapport as I discussed my needs for creative writing and believe it or not, she had a solution. She invited me to her creative writing group— Flamingo Authors. This is yet another of her attempts to help coax the hidden creativity in many of us. The only pre condition to joining the group was, 'you will have to have begun writing your epoch-making creative tome'. She is persuasive, encouraging and believes passionately in a creative sisterhood. I was, at that stage, too mentally lazy to give a form and shape to my creative fantasies and therefore held back.

But I followed the activities of the creative group. Many of the members began writing their short stories or novels and here is Anne, true to her promise, with her first book.

The first had to be in the self-help genre because that is how she is—always willing to lend a helping hand to anyone who needs it.

She has promised to create a series in this genre and knowing her determination you can expect the rest soon. As someone who has gone through this important rite of passage to be a somewhat seasoned expatriate, I look forward to including the series in my collection of 'must-haves' in my personal library.

I think there is nothing more comforting and empowering than settling down to good read and sharing a rewarding anecdote about how someone like yourself happened to grow roots in Dubai.

Suchitra Bajpai Chaudhary, senior feature writer, *Gulf News, Friday Magazine*

Introduction

Contemplating a move to a new city in a totally foreign part of the world where you've never been before? What's the first thing you should do?

"Spend as much time as possible researching your new home location and office environment. Go online and learn as much as you can about both the country and its people."

I couldn't have said it better myself. This great piece of advice comes from Victoria Hepworth and Andrea Martin in *Expat Women: Confessions – 50 Answers to your Real-Life Questions about Living Abroad*.

Whether it's your first or fiftieth expat experience, there's going to be anxiety. So arm yourself with good insider information and be assured that you're not alone.

Where do you begin? How do you make it feel like home? How do you get connected? The *@Home in* guides provide newcomers and vagabonders, laptop entrepreneurs and busman's holidaymakers the complete how-to guide on getting connected in a foreign city. Starting with the resources that are available right at your fingertips, through the keyboard of your computer, each edition of *@ Home in* focuses on a specific city and/or country.

An expat's best friend is the Internet. It is like a box of caramel corn. Lots of sweet stuff; interspersed with a little crunch to make you stop and think; a few un-popped kernels like incomplete thoughts that need some mulling over; and finally a surprise that gives you exactly what you're looking for.

The *@Home in* guides provide you with insider information and Internet resources to help you cut through the quagmire quickly and home in on the best resources and online references. These have been provided by expats who have been there before and done the work for you. It's sure to save you endless time and trouble.

@Home in Dubai… Getting Connected Online and on the Ground is the first in the series.

Personality Traits of Successful Expats

But first, have you considered if you have the fortitude for expat living? Do you think you are born with the ability to adapt to new people and places or is it a learned response? I believe it's a combination of both.

My husband, Doug, always says I'm like a cat. You can toss me up in the air and, no matter what; I always land on my feet. I like to think all us expats are like that. We're nimble, tolerant, open-minded and adventurous. An expat needs to be able to make a home anywhere.

Here's a little kernel to munch on. Maria Foley @ Iwasanexpatwife, blogs about 'The Big 5 Personality Traits' required to survive and enjoy the expat experience. Here's an excerpt from Maria's blog (with her permission):

"The Big Five traits have been found to be relatively stable across the life span, and are consistent in relation to sex, age, and culture. What's interesting from an intercultural perspective is that they're being used to predict the success of managers on expatriate assignments (and to a much lesser extent, the success of tag-along family members).

Why should this matter to the expat spouse? One recent study hailed personality variables as 'the strongest determinants of cultural adjustment of expatriate spouses'. It stands to reason that if there's a correlation between certain personality characteristics and success in a social or cultural environment, your life will be a helluva lot easier if you're the lucky owner of those particular traits."

The Big Five personality dimensions are:

- <u>Agreeableness</u>
- <u>Conscientiousness</u>
- <u>Extraversion</u>
- <u>Neuroticism</u>
- <u>Openness to experience</u>

More details on these traits can be found on Maria's blog at http://iwasanexpatwife.com.

You can take the Big Five Personality Test yourself at www.outofservice.com/bigfive. In her blog, Maria admits that she failed it miserably but went on to thoroughly enjoy her expat experience (she's now repatriated to Canada). By the way, Maria is not just a blogger… she has a master's degree in intercultural communications from Royal Roads University in Victoria, British Columbia (Canada) and wrote her masters thesis on the value of cross-cultural training for expat spouses.

Now, don't lose hope if you feel you are lacking one or more of these traits. Just recognize that you might have to work a little harder to adjust and that's why @*Home in* is here to help.

I first became an expat in 1993 when Doug and I escaped the cold Canadian winter for the glorious year-round warmth of sunny South Florida. Known as 'snowbirds', Canadians have been doing this for years. In 1992, a new category of work visa opened up with the North American Free Trade Agreement (NAFTA) between Canada, the US and Mexico that welcomed anyone with a specialized bachelors degree. So, with my bachelor of public relations in hand, off we went. Doug was working for Air Canada based in Toronto at the time, so his plan was to commute from Florida, which he did for 14 years.

What triggered this adventure was a book Doug found online called *The Border Guide* by Robert Keats. The written word often inspires people to try something completely different and now that written word is so much more easily accessible online. Learning from other people's experiences and picturing yourself in the same scenario is so helpful.

It wasn't such a drastic change for us to move from Canada to the US but our next move from the US to Dubai was much more complicated. I wish there had been an *@Home in Dubai* then. It would have saved me some sleepless nights. That's what the *@Home in* guides are all about.

Having lived in Dubai, one of the seven Emirates in the United Arab Emirates (UAE), from 2007 to 2011 and having assisted others with the settling in process, I have journeyed many times through the steps needed to make Dubai your home. *@Home in Dubai... Getting Connected Online and on the Ground*, will help you explore how to settle into life in Dubai. I welcome you to the city I grew very fond of, and hope that the information contained herein proves helpful.

Get ready to meet Dubai... "The city of captivating contrasts"... aptly named by Dubai Tourism.

Dubai's Expat Community

The expat community in Dubai is an eclectic patchwork of people. It is impossible to identify a typical profile. There are the families with Third Culture Kids (TCKs) who grow up in Dubai and graduate from one of the many expat schools; singles seeking their fortunes as upwardly mobile professionals; entrepreneurs with creative new business ideas; and newly married and empty nest couples looking to combine employment with a great adventure. Dubai's expats come from every imaginable part of the world; some places you may even hear of for the first time.

Dubai offers tremendous opportunities but not without the potential for some serious pitfalls. In any expat community, there are examples of amazing success stories and heart wrenching disappointments. But, that's life, isn't it? Sometimes you just have to hold your nose and jump in. So, before you take the plunge, take a deep breath and let me help you get connected with Dubai online and on the ground.

@*Home in Dubai* Survey Respondents

Of all the generous people who responded to the @*Home in Dubai* survey about half were first time expats and half were seasoned veterans, which means there are plenty of rich experiences to share. Our veteran expats have lived all over the world: Malaysia, Borneo, Hong Kong, Saudi Arabia, Germany, Belgium, Holland, Honduras, Japan, Italy, UK, US, Canada, Sudan, Uganda, Tanzania, Tunisia, Russia, Sweden, India, Cambodia, Jordan, Kuwait, Bahrain, Sierra Leone, Singapore, Norway, Indonesia, France, Spain, The Netherlands, Hungary, Papua New Guinea, Thailand and China.

A majority are trailing spouses (or STARS, Spouse Traveling And Relocating Successfully, as we like to call them now) and others moved to Dubai for a change, adventure or to make the 'big bucks'.

"At that time (30 years ago) Dubai beckoned like a Shangri-La; it was considered a great place to live. Besides, my husband got this great job here," says Padmini Sankar, a long-time Indian expat.

"I was approached by a head-hunter whom had been a friend for years back in the UK," said Alba Micheli Geddes from Italy. "There was a job which apparently had my name on it and was I interested in coming to Dubai? I was immediately intrigued and interested and started reading about Dubai and the UAE. I was flown out in August 2008 for an interview and got to visit the city for three days. I was subsequently offered the job and my employer took care of the logistics of moving me here."

Karen Beggs from Northern Ireland says she came for the better salary and tax-free income and thought it would be great to live in a nicer climate. "I guess I wanted an adventure, wanted something more than I felt I could have at home," said Karen. And Dubai was the place that had it all.

"We always wanted to live in an Arab country and we'd had enough of London and wanted somewhere safe and exciting to raise a family," adds Ed Capaldi from Italy.

The reasons for moving to Dubai are as varied as its multi-cultural fabric.

"I wanted to live somewhere near my parents who are based in Yemen and so Dubai seemed like the perfect location with only a two-hour and 20-minute flight to Yemen," shares Dhuha, a British/Yemini. "At the same time, westernised enough for us to fit in as a mixed couple and with a Middle Eastern touch that I craved to experience again."

Some expats came as kids with their parents and never left.

"I moved to Dubai when I was two and a half years old in 1977," says British expat Marissa Woods, personal brand expert and entrepreneur. "My parents came here because my father worked as a senior executive in the oil business and my mother a teacher, restarted her teaching career in Dubai with teaching English to graduates and businessmen, as there were no schools when we arrived!"

Tip

"Planning is critical. That initial gush of wide-eyed joy will dissipate as daily routines set in and, as it does, aspects of this new society will grate so be prepared."

Paul Allen, author, *Should I Stay or Should I Go.*

Chapter 1

Connecting – with Authorities and Services Legally

Work Permits and Residence Visas

These two little gems go hand in hand but the work permit must come first. You can't get a residence visa without a work permit or by being sponsored by someone who has one (a spouse, parent, son or daughter). The experiences are a real mixed bag. There are new laws being bandied about that will give those investing in real estate a residence visa but the details are vague (read more in *Chapter 5, Buying a Property*).

A good rule of thumb is to have work lined up before you come to Dubai, as your employer will typically handle the process of getting approval through the Ministry of Labour for you to work. Once you have your work permit and labour card, then you (or your company on your behalf) will submit a request to the Department of Naturalization and Residency of Dubai (DNRD) for a residence visa.

As Doug was the one with the job offer, I waited in Canada until all his paperwork was complete and he had applied for (and received) my temporary residence visa, based on his sponsorship.

My mom was thrilled by the extended visit. One day I was pacing around the house, waiting for Doug to call with an update. It had been about a month.

"Don't worry," my mom said trying to placate me. "There's no rush. Stay as long as you like."

I knew she was just trying to help, but I had to turn away so she wouldn't see the angst written all over my face. There's nothing worse than being in limbo and, as much as I adore my mom, I just wanted to get my new life underway. I was missing my husband terribly.

In the grand scheme of things, it worked out pretty well. A few days later, Doug got word that my temporary visa had been approved. A couple of days after that, my flight on Emirates was booked.

Once I arrived in Dubai, a representative from *Marhaba* met me when I got off the flight with my permit in hand. Doug had arranged for that ahead of time. In order to enter as a resident, I had to have the original in hand when going through immigration and there hadn't been time to courier it. Doug couldn't come through security but the *Marhaba* folks could.

I highly recommend this service, especially if it's your first time to Dubai (www.marhabaservices.com). It's available at all terminals at the Dubai International Airport and they escort you to all right places and you move to the front of the queue in customs and immigration. After a 14-hour flight, arriving at night in a strange place, the smiling lady dressed in a bright yellow blazer, holding a sign with my name on it was a welcome sight.

Gather Documentation Before you leave

Depending on what your profession is, there may be a few extra documents needed that you wouldn't expect. Knowing about them in advance saves a lot of time, aggravation and money. Also note that some documents will need to be translated and attested.

"The best place I have found is the Roads and Transport Authority (RTA) Al Barsha offices on the Sheikh Zayed Road next to the Dubai Gold and Diamond Park by the Mall of Emirates. Documents such as your marriage licence or driver's licence are quickly translated for a nominal fee by a very polite Emirati gentleman," says Katie Foster in her blog, '8 Tips to Survive Your Move to Dubai' at http://arabiantalesandotheramazingadventures. blogspot.com.

As you prepare to leave your home country have about 30 passport-sized photos taken and keep them on you at all times. You'll understand why as you read on.

"Before you arrive make sure that your passport is renewed, as many companies won't give you a visa if your passport is to expire in 12 months," was some good advice Gillian from South Africa offered. It always amazes me when we travel somewhere and even a visit visa requires at least six months remaining on your passport. What's the point of an expiration date if the actual 'expiration' is six months before the date showing? But these fussy details can make or break your transition… or at least make it more difficult than it needs to be if you're not aware of the requirements.

"I had to have my degree documents legalised and attested in Australia and provide my passport and a number of passport photos and send them to my company in Dubai before I could leave Australia to start my role," says Kara Boden who works in the finance industry.

She's gone through the process twice now and shares, "This is my second job in Dubai and my visa processing has always taken longer than anticipated. I had decided to move onto my husband's visa and I am currently on a tourist visa while my husband's company continues to sort it out seven weeks after my last one was cancelled."

Make sure you give yourself enough time to usher all your documents through the relevant government agencies. If you're on top of it, chances are it will go smoothly. Scottish expat Jonathan Castle had a bit of a nightmare experience when somewhere along the line his degree and diploma certificate were lost and he had to get replacements of each. "These were then notarised by the issuing institution, attested by the Foreign Office and the UAE Embassy in London, then couriered here and attested again by the British Consulate, the British Council and the UAE Labour Department, before being approved by the DNRD. Seven stamps!" says Jonathan. "It's like playing a game of chess only they don't tell you the rules until after you've made a mistake."

We jumped through the same hoops during the interview and job offer process with Doug's credentials being scrutinised and verified. Fortunately Doug found out by chance before he left Canada that we would also need our marriage licence attested in Ottawa as well before I could come. It was part of the documentation required for Doug to submit my residence visa application.

Although I waited in Canada for my residence visa to be finalised, many spouses choose not to and enter on a visitor's visa that's good for 30 days. In most cases this is enough time to procure your residence visa if sponsored by a spouse that already has a work permit. If it takes longer (like Kara's did) you may have to do a 'visa run' to a neighbouring country (usually Oman) but the rules on that change regularly so check to make sure if that's at all possible before you make that your game plan.

As cautionary note, I think it's better for spouse and children to wait to relocate until the work permit and residence visa have been secured. There are numerous stories about entire families moving to Dubai before everything was finalised and a few months later having to move the entire family back home again as the permit hadn't come through for some reason.

"If a company sponsors you, they take care of everything. Otherwise, it can be tricky and there are lots of unexpected curveballs that pop up," says Jeanette Todd from Canada. "My first residence visa was done by my employer. The second time, through a free zone as my sponsor, was challenging, as there were many delays and trips to the immigration department. Everything takes at least three tries to get accomplished."

Some companies will have a public relations officer (PRO) on staff that is responsible for facilitating the residence visa process. If you're managing it yourself it's not a bad idea to hire a PRO. As with any profession, some are better than others.

"I tend to recommend a relocation company here, which does so much more than just what a PRO does, and that company is *Executive Expatriate Relocations* (http://dubaimoving.com)," said Greg Pogonowski an independent financial adviser based in Dubai.

"This can be a total nightmare depending on your PRO," said marketing specialist Fiona Thomas from Scotland who has provided these services herself. "You need a PRO to assist you as there are so many variations (of residence permit) involved. Be sure to get all his details and a copy of his passport just in case. Mistakes are made very easily," said Fiona. "Typically a PRO will tell you everything is okay when it isn't. But that's true in general in Dubai. For any questions, there is a 24/7 Ministry of Labour number, 800 665, which is an excellent service. Department of Naturalization and Residency is also great for advice, www.dnrd.ae."

"My company did all the paperwork, I had to give something like 16 photos, had a medical consisting of a blood test and a chest x-ray. I then gave my passport to the PRO in our company and in three days my visa appeared as by magic," says Italian Alba Micheli Geddes.

Some companies are more efficient at arranging work permits and residency visas than others. It often depends on the relationship the company has with the respective government departments, which could explain the wide range of experiences shared by survey respondents.

"The residence visa was handled by my work. I had it easy but there are many friends that I know in Dubai that have waited months to get their visa from their employers," says Canadian expat Mary-Alison Lyman.

Contrary to Jeanette's experience, sometimes getting your residence visa through a free zone is a breeze. "I handed a check in to Knowledge Village Business Centre and they did the rest," says Debbie Nicol, creator of *embers of the world* and managing director of *business en motion*.

Beware of Limitations

It's important to be aware that there are age limitations when applying for work permits in the UAE. If you are over 60 your application will be turned down, unless you have a highly specialized skill and there is a senior corporate or government official who will lobby the DNRD to waive the age restriction on your behalf.

Also if you are a female trailing spouse, you can work but there's another little piece of paper you'll need which states that your husband gives you permission to work.

"It was easy in the sense that my residency visa was sponsored by my husband, so his company facilitated the process," said Amy from Canada. "Both companies for which I've worked required a 'No Objection' letter from my husband before they would extend a job offer to me. They also both offered to sponsor my residency, but I have chosen to remain on my husband's sponsorship."

Of course, I knew I would want to work at some point so when we heard that I would need a letter of permission from my husband, Doug asked me how many copies I'd like. I kept an electronic copy of his signature so I could update the letter whenever I needed it.

If you are a male trailing spouse it's important to note that a wife can only sponsor her husband if she is in a particular profession (and the list is short). She must be a teacher, doctor, engineer or 'equivalent' (ambiguous, I know) and must have a minimum salary of AED 5,000 per month. There are some reports that there is flexibility on acceptable occupations if the wife is earning more than AED 10,000, but check with DNRD for updates.

The Ideal Scenario

If you have a job offer prior to coming to Dubai, companies will often apply in advance for a temporary residence permit for you, which allows you to enter the country and is valid for 30 days. During this time, the company will submit the paperwork for a residence visa that is usually valid for three years (as long as you're not outside of the country for a period of longer than six months at any given time).

The rules do tend to change periodically so updates can be found online at http://www.dubaifaqs.com/visa-dubai.php. On the homepage it even says right upfront, "Visa rules and requirements can and do change suddenly, and without warning. The UAE embassy in your country or the relevant authority in the UAE (DNRD) is probably the only source of information you can rely on... even government websites can be slow to update."

All residence applications also require a medical report including blood tests and chest x-rays.

"My husband's company took care of this for me. A very nice gentleman took some of the other wives and me to a medical facility to get our blood drawn so we could get our visas. Once there, he drew numbers for us which we quickly learned meant nothing. Something like a bargaining and negotiating process ensued in order to determine who would go next in the small room crowded with at least 50 people. Being from the United States, I was used to a good deal of privacy regarding any medical procedure. I was quite shocked that at least 20 people were looking on through the open doorway as I got my blood drawn. It was really unnerving," said American Shirley W Ralston.

The Practicalities

Documents to prepare for work permit:

- Valid passport (at least 6 months left before expiry date) for all family members.

- Attested/certified education certificate (or degree) in country of issue.

- If you are the female spouse, a no objection letter from your husband.

Documents for residency permit for yourself and family members:

- Passport copies (bring originals for verification).

- Two passport photos for each family member.

- Attested marriage certificate from your home country.

- Divorce decree (if you've been married before).

- Children's school records (official transfer certificate from previous school/s).

- Vaccination records for all family members.

- Birth certificates (long form is preferable).

- Medical test results (including x-rays and blood tests as anyone with HIV/Aids, TB or hepatitis B will not admitted into the UAE).

- Company trade licence (if you're setting up your own business) or Ministry of Labour work permit approval.

The Five –Step Recap

Step 1

Get a firm job offer.

Step 2

Go to a registered typing office to have application forms for work permit completed (in Arabic). If you haven't arrived in Dubai yet, your company will probably take care of this. If you are handling this yourself, here is a list of typing centres in Dubai: http://www.eida.gov.ae/en/process-and-fees/registration-plan.aspx Most typing centres will do any translation you need as well (sometimes required for university degree documents and driving licences from some countries).

Step 3

Authorised company representative submits application and supporting documentation to DNRD either at the post office or official typing centre (if you are taking care of this yourself take your documents and the application form that the typing centre has prepared for you to any post office, place them in a 'labour envelope' and *Empost* will send to DNRD). You can check the status on the web portal www.DNRD.ae. Once approved, either your

PRO will pick it up or you can retrieve it at the post office indicated on the approval notice (notification is usually sent via SMS). The approval document is used to secure your employment visa and, in some instances, a labour card is issued. The work permit allows you to enter the country and then begin the residence visa process. If you're already in the country this will enable you to convert your visit visa to a residence visa.

Step 4

Get health checks and blood tests (your sponsor should tell you which approved medical clinic to go to). You'll need to show your employment permit and provide... guess what... two more passport sized photos.

Step 5

Apply for residence visa by repeating steps 2 and 3 with DNRD Residence Section application forms (must take place within 60 days of arrival in Dubai). Once visa is obtained, submit application for family members under your sponsorship.

Note: The three-year residence visa is renewable if you have continual employment. Student residence visas and domestic help residence visas are only valid for one year.

Tip

A list of authorized typing centres can be found on the Emirates Identity Authority website at http://www.eida.gov.ae/en/process-and-fees/registration-plan.aspx If you decide you need to hire a PRO, they will get the required application forms and handle typing and translation for you. Try to get a referral from a colleague or friend. As a last resort do a Google search for 'PRO services Dubai'.

Case Study #1

"My work visa was arranged through work. I actually had a trip out of the country, to Italy with my mother, about a month and a half after I arrived. There was a moment where I was told that my passport wouldn't be ready for that trip. Someone from work had submitted it to visa authorities and was unsure if it would be ready. Thankfully it all worked out but I learned my lesson quickly that you have to stay on top of people and be sure that pressure is put on. Otherwise there is a chance no progress will be made."

Mary-Alison Lyman, Canadian

Case Study #2

"The residence visa process was handled by my husband's work and a so-called PRO who handles visa applications for companies and their employees. Nevertheless, the process was delayed. This will either cost a fine (paid by the company) or a drive to Oman and back... we chose the latter. We left for Oman (a one and a half hour drive) and came back with fresh stamps in our passports! Then the procedure started all over again; this time, with one more delay and a fine. It took us three months to get valid visas."

Vibeke Nurgberg, Danish National

The Wrap up

The most confusing part of securing your residence visa and work permit is that there are so many ways of doing both and such a litany of different categories that it makes your head spin. In order to keep your wits about you (when all about you are losing theirs) maintain a gracious attitude and carry copies of everything with you everywhere you go. My mother always told me you get more bees with honey, so approach every situation with a smile (even if you're gritting your teeth behind it). The To Do list is overwhelming at first but as you check each item off, give yourself a pat on the back and move on to the next one.

I know my fingers itch with excitement whenever I can scratch something off the list, even though it sometimes seems it's getting longer.

Chapter 2

Getting a Bank Account

The good news is that there are numerous banks to choose from and many that you might recognise from your home country like *Citibank*, www.citibank.com/uae, *HSBC*, www.hsbc.ae, and the *Royal Bank of Scotland*, www. rbsbank.ae.

On the ground, you may not find any signs for cabarets or cocktail lounges along the main drags of Al Wasl and Jumeirah Beach Road (don't forget, you are in a Muslim country), but there are copious billboards and banners touting the latest financial services. There's a bank practically on every block but some of them are 'business centres' and the type of banking you can do there is limited. In 2009, *Emirates Bank* and *National Bank of Dubai* merged into one *Emirates NBD* bank (www.emiratesnbd. com) so the yellow and blue brand is everywhere.

As always, you can do plenty of preliminary research online to see the litany of banks on offer (personal, commercial, investment or Islamic banking) and determine where the closest branch is. A great place to start is www.

guide2dubai.com that has an extensive list of authorised banking institutions. For commercial or investment banking the *Dubai International Financial Centre* (www. DIFC.ae) is a great resource as well.

"Personally, I use *Lloyds TSB* (www.lloydstsb.ae) and for the business we use *Abu Dhabi Commercial Bank* (ADCB) (www.adcb.com). Both accounts were fairly easy to set up," says Claire Fenner, co-founder of women's entrepreneurial network, *Heels & Deals.*

Finding a branch close to where you're living or working is going to be important, as there will often be a need to appear in person to resolve an issue that you're probably used to handling online. Another consideration is to deal with the same bank that the company paycheque is issued by. Although all banks claim to have online access make sure you 'test-drive' the customer interface before making any commitments. Dubai is a face-to-face place and even though there are the trappings of technology, it has its fair share of glitches. There seems to be a preference to resolve your concerns at the branch.

Most banks will also require that your paycheque be deposited into your account each month in order to issue you a credit card according to American expat and blogger Pam Rollings. "My husband uses *HSBC* and has found the banking to be quite difficult. They will not issue him a credit card as he refuses to deposit his paycheque in Dubai but has it deposited in his Pittsburgh bank account. This has caused us problems as you need a local credit card to pay for most utilities online, so we have to pay many of our bills in person."

Each bank has its own idiosyncrasies and once you get to know them… just be prepared for them to change.

Doug and I started with *Mashreq* (www.mashreqbank.com) but weren't happy with the service so switched to *Emirates NBD*. Unfortunately, we switched during the merger so had to manage two accounts simultaneously while they sorted out the administrative melding. What we have discovered is that, as with most customer service oriented industries, the efficiency of the service is directly related to the person you're dealing with and how much they care about their job and their customers.

"Customer service at all banks in Dubai in general isn't great. As long as you're employed in a company that is registered with them everything is easy. The moment you're on your own and have your own business this is where it gets impossible. There should definitely be more financial support for SME's in this country," says Rawan Albina, wife, mother and professional certified coach from Lebanon.

The tide does seem to be changing especially since Small and Medium Enterprises (SMEs) are a big part of the UAE economy. "In Dubai, the country's trade and tourism hub, SMEs contribute to at least half of the emirate's economic output and employ around two-thirds of its estimated 1.4 million workforce", according to an *Arabian Business*

Magazine article on March 22, 2011 titled 'UAE banks failing to back entrepreneurs'.

"To open a corporate account is very lengthy process, as it becomes just another stage of the company licence setup. It can be tricky as the licence setup gives you a paper that you must take to the bank, then the licence setup waits for the bank to contact them, and won't restart until you carry a document from the bank back to your licence setup people," says Debbie Nicol, creator of *embers of the world* and managing director of *business en motion*.

There's the odd person who seems quite content with their bank. British expat Beryl Comar, an EQ (emotional IQ) development specialist and owner of *The Change Associates* in Dubai, uses *Commercial Bank of Dubai* (www.cbd.ae) and says they have "easy and wonderful service". And, she's been banking with them for 27 years. Talk about loyalty!

Italian expat, Alba Micheli Geddes, had similarly good luck with her banking. "It was all very easy as my employer set me up with a choice of two banks. I chose *HSBC* and a representative came to my office and did all the necessary paperwork. Within days I had an account, a cash card and two credit cards," she says.

Sometimes your employer will smooth out the process for you. However, if you are a woman under your husband's sponsorship, you will have to jump through a few more hoops to open your own bank account. If you don't have the requisite salary letter, in some cases you'll have to maintain a minimum balance. You can have a 'joint account' but make sure you ask what that means.

Doug and I opened a joint account. One day I attempted to do some phone banking.

"I'm sorry but you don't have phone access to this account," said the gentleman on the other end of the line.

"But I know my husband set it up. I can give you the password if you like," I answered trying to keep the irritation out of my voice.

"Your husband has access. You do not," he replied matter-of-factly.

"But it's a joint account."

"I'm sorry but you'll have to come in to the branch to make these changes. You don't have phone banking access," he insisted.

"I'll have to speak to my husband."

"Hmm."

I hung up. I was apoplectic. But there was nothing to do about it. I resolved myself to the fact that, after 20 years of keeping track of my own finances, I would be handing all control back to Doug. *One-one-thousand, two-one-thousand, three-one-thousand...* inhale, exhale.

Ask lots of questions, but always expect the unexpected because you are in a different part of the world. The penalty for bouncing a check is jail time. As a practice, I don't write cheques. The one cheque I did write in Dubai was returned because my signature didn't *exactly* match the one they had on file. Are you kidding me? What a pain. So... I just stopped writing cheques. It was cash or cheque card for me.

Actually, once I got off the phone from this frustrating conversation I headed out the door into a crystal blue day, the sun shining bright and the birds singing from the palm trees swaying in my front yard. I walked a short 15 minutes to a secluded beach nestled between two palaces. I have no idea who lives in them but it must be someone pretty important. One of them looks like Ali Baba's palace. I walked onto the glimmering white, powdery sand under the watchful eye of the Burj Al Arab, the only seven-star hotel in the world, and smiled. This isn't so bad. I can let Doug deal with the bank.

The Practicalities

Once you do choose a bank, here is a list of documents you will need in order for you to open your account (as you get yourself set up, be ready to produce this list of documents for practically anything you want to do):

- Passport copies including residence visa page (for both parties if it's a joint account). Bring the original as well since the bank will have to actually see it to verify that it's legitimate.

- Two passport sized photos (double check as some banks may require two for the account application and two for the credit card application).

- A letter from your company confirming regular employment (a salary letter).

- A copy of your lease or rental agreement (some banks ask for this, some don't).

- Some banks will require one (or more) forms of local ID like a driving licence or a utility bill.

The Five-Step Recap

Step 1

Research banks in your immediate area.

Step 2

Choose one that provides the services you need.

Step 3

Test-run the online interface.

Step 4

Make sure you have all the necessary documents.

Step 5

Submit the application in person (and follow up daily). Check bank hours before you go as the times vary dramatically from bank to bank and branch to branch, some closing as early as one o'clock in the afternoon.

Tip

Always have plenty of colour passport photos on hand at all times. Everywhere you go the first couple of months to set up anything from a bank account to getting your driving licence will require two photos and sometimes more.

Case Study #1

"For us setting up a bank account was horrific! It took over three months. One problem is that there is no home mail delivery in the UAE and my husband works on a construction site and they (*HSBC*) kept trying to deliver documents and cards to him and couldn't find his office. I simply had to call every day until delivery was finally made. And, we were unable to get a credit card without an extremely hefty deposit in a special account because we are over 60. To make it worse, all accounts are in Roger's name so I have to carry a 'no objection letter' from him giving permission for me to handle the account. I just keep the letter on my computer and print them out changing the name of the company as needed and sign them. This always resolves the issue although a little tough to do by phone."

Katie Foster, American blogger and freelance writer

Case Study #2

"Banking is certainly one area where the horror stories of Dubai are real. We have had money go missing during transfers and had to fight for months for its return. A friend had her credit card stolen, and even with a police report, the bank blamed her for the fraudulent transactions. We've endured endless red tape and delays for the simplest transactions and countless hours on the phone and in the branch trying to set up services or rectify errors. We are required to complete inane procedures and paperwork for things that would be automatic in other jurisdictions. We have been here three and a half years and have switched banks three times to no avail."

Amy, Canadian

The Wrap up

Processes and procedures in Dubai change on a daily basis. As a young centre for commerce it often has growing pains, but you have to stand back and watch in awe at what's been accomplished in such a short time. This applies very much to the banking system. There are programmes being introduced every day to streamline the process for small and medium enterprises and for women as well. In the book *Dubai The Journey* by Pranay Gupte, Sheikh Mohammed is quoted as saying, "I like to think that Dubai is unlike any other Arabian centre that has risen from a hostile desert in barely a decade to become an unusual model of social harmony and sustainable development, one where capitalism is constantly being reinvented and refined, and where opportunities for personal prosperity are continually being expanded."

Chapter 3

Budget Accommodation – Short-Term/ Long-Term

It seems every day you see a new compound or apartment complex or apartment hotel sprouting up from behind a construction barrier. Construction has slowed down but there's still a hum of activity, the roads continue to be busy and mall parking lots are full to capacity. It's part two of the 'Field of Dreams'. If you build it they will come. And, they do. So, there are lots of housing options to choose from.

Everyone has a different way of attacking a chore. No matter what your style is, it's best to approach this animal in a methodical way, or you'll literally be driving around in circles.

"I would recommend dedicating two full days on the search to just identify an area in Dubai that could suit and start looking," says Italian expat, Alba Micheli Geddes. "I find sites like *Dubizzle* (www.dubizzle.com) really useful. On top of that you have loads of real estate agents eager to get your business."

For the short-term, Rawan Albina says, "There are lots of budget hotels in town now. These didn't exist five years ago. Rates online are much better than when you book in person here."

Checking online first is a good start (try www.cheaperthanhotels.ae as well as *Dubizzle*) but make sure you combine that with personal references from people who have experienced it first hand. "*Dubizzle* is a marvel for accommodation but the best thing is to find someone who lives here and ask them questions. Even if you don't know anyone here, someone in your network will and most expats will take a call from a newcomer," says Dawn from Ireland.

I've seen loads of hotel/apartments around town so there's no shortage of temporary accommodation. The beauty of it being temporary means that even if it's not perfect, it's not forever. A great online resource that has a huge long list of serviced apartments is www.expatechodubai.com. In the search window on the home page, type in 'serviced apartments directory'. But sometimes it's best to start with a shorter list from others' recommendations. There were several specific recommendations given by survey respondents such as:

- *Radisson Blu* in the marina, www.radissonblu.com/hotel-dubaimarina, for short-term, shared by Rikke Ebel Nielsen from Denmark who lives at the Marina (it's probably not particularly cheap but I guess it depends on what you consider 'budget').

- Brands such as *Easyhotel*, <u>www.easyhotel.com/ hotels/dubai</u>, that have now set up in Dubai, a recommendation from freelance writer and Brit, Karen Osman (more short versus long-term).

- *Belvedere Court* in Bur Dubai or *Crystal Living Court* in TECOM, <u>http://dubai.pro-stay.com/ dubai_apartments/crystal-living-court</u>, for short or long-term budget accommodation, Danish national, Vibeke Nurgberg suggests.

- *Media Rotana* – Al Barsha, <u>www.rotana.com/rotanahotelandresorts/ unitedarabemirates/dubai/mediarotana</u>

Often times a newcomer may be looking for shared accommodations. "For a single person looking for short-term budget accommodation, I would recommend living with others. I did this for a while and it was great to meet others from a variety of cultures," said Karen Beggs from Northern Ireland. "For a couple, I would suggest that they do a bit of research and go and see a lot of buildings. There are now bargains in Dubai and I would advise that people NEVER accept the first price as everything is negotiable."

Negotiating for anything is a sport in Dubai, whether you're at one of the many souks or searching for a place to live. It's finally a renter's market so even with long-term stay hotels you can probably get a discounted rate for several weeks or months.

"Negotiate a weekly or monthly rate with one of the more modest hotels along Sheikh Zayed Road like the *Ibis* or *Holiday Inn* near the Mall of the Emirates," suggests Amy from Canada. "They're close to the metro, not too sleazy and central to many things."

"My suggestion… consider being near the Metro if that mode of transportation is important to you," said Katie Foster, American blogger and freelance writer.

Additional Recommendations for Budget Accommodation:

- *International City*, www.internationalcity.ae, is definitely more long-term. It's further out of town, but close to Dragon Mart, a popular discount mall where all the merchandise is imported from China.

- *Al Marooj Rotana Hotel and Suites*, www.rotana.com, has daily, weekly and monthly rates with one and two bedroom suites that include living areas.

- *Galleria Apartments*, www.thegalleria.hyatt.com, at the *Hyatt Regency* is in Deira, an older part of town, near the Dubai Creek. It has one, three, six and 12-month rental periods available with one to five bedroom units.

- *Golden Sands Hotel Apartments*, www. goldensandsdubai.com, received several votes on the *@Home in Dubai* survey. It's in Bur Dubai near Burjuman Shopping Mall. Of course, no matter where you are in Dubai, there's a shopping centre close by.

- *Oasis Centre*, www.oasisbeachtower.com, at Dubai Marina, a newer part of town, has one, two and three-bedroom apartments.

- *Trade Centre Apartments*, www.dwtc.com, is right in the downtown core near the financial district so probably on the high side cost-wise, but it has one, two and three-bedroom apartments available for daily, weekly, monthly and yearly rates.

- *Premier Inn*, www.global.premierinn.com, near Dubai Investment Park is more for short-term verses a long-term stay.

- *Crowne Plaza*, *Chelsea Tower* and *Radisson Blu* (recommended by an Expats Living in Dubai *Facebook* group member).

- *Gloria Hotel*, www.gloriahoteldubai.com, in Media City, has one and two bedroom apartments for a longer-term stay.

I actually receive regular emails of seasonal specials at local hotels (not that I was an appropriate target until I started writing this book, but I guess they hoped I would forward to visiting friends). One example of a group of budget accommodations I received was *ETA Star Hospitality* (www.etastarhospitality.com) that has several locations around town. It looks like it's worth checking into.

The Practicalities

- If you're looking at short-term temporary accommodation in a hotel/apartment, a work visa and/or residence permit won't be necessary but the hotel will probably ask for a passport copy.

- If you need temporary accommodation for more than 30 days be prepared to show a passport with either a multiple-entry business visa or a longer-term residence visa.

The Five-Step Recap

Step 1

Do the preliminary online research and collect recommendations from friends and colleagues.

Step 2

Check out the websites of the hotel/apartments listed here.

Step 3

If you need to hire an agent to do an advance search before you arrive or you'd just rather not pound the pavement yourself, check out www.bhomes.com or www. moveoneinc.com.

Step 4

Choose an area that is fairly central so you can explore all areas of Dubai while you hunt for your permanent accommodation.

Step 5

Start the search for your final home.

> **Tip**
>
> For short-term accommodation there's a great website to visit to get an idea of the range of hotel options available in Dubai (or anywhere else in the world). Check out www.booking.com and type in Dubai in the city search window on the home page, the dates you need and the number of people. You can filter your search based on other needs as well such as price range and amenities.

Case Study #1

"There are now so many serviced apartments, especially in the Barsha area. Additionally, there are some great three-star properties like the Centro brand of *Rotana*. I would suggest to newcomers to take a hotel for one week and look to relocate to some family suites for the rest of the 'looking around' time. I just visited a friend who'd relocated and spent her first four months in *Fraser Suites* on Sheikh Zayed Road (near Knowledge Village). It has fantastic amenities and is well worth the look."

Aussie expat Debbie Nicol, creator of *embers of the world* and managing director of *business en motion*

Case Study #2

"I have heard really great things about the *Gulf Pearl* in Al Barsha. The management is very good. It's run by *Dusit Hotels*. I have a work colleague who has lived there for about a year and loves it. The cost is approximately AED 12,000 to 15,000 per month, which isn't too bad for what you get when you do the comparisons. There's another one opposite called *Executive Hotel*. It has good food, a nice restaurant and great amenities and another great manager running the place."

Fiona Thomas, marketing consultant from Scotland

The Wrap up

Whatever area of Dubai you choose, there are going to be pros and cons because there's such diversity. If you like wide, open spaces, you'll have to choose a spot somewhere a little outside of town. The city itself is congested by rows and rows of architectural wonders. It can be fun to drive around town taking it all in, while speculating how in the world they ever constructed a building with so many twists and turns or if that tallest building in the world sways when you get to the top. You won't wind up there for your short or long-term budget accommodation, but it's fun to look at and imagine what it might be like to live there and rub elbows with the likes of Giorgio Armani.

Chapter 4

Renting a Property

We were lucky when we moved to Dubai. Doug was hired by Emirates Airline, which has an employee assistance centre where employees and their spouses and children can go to get advice, direction and assistance on everything from getting your driver's licence to applying for your 'alcoholics drinks licence'. I know… it's a funny name. I guess all of us who enjoy the odd libation must be alcoholics… (by the way, you apply for it at any *Maritime and Mercantile International* store, better known as *MMI*, www.mmidubai.com, but you need a letter from your company). But I digress.

Another welcome benefit that Emirates Airline employees enjoy is company accommodation, which is actually quite nice. The company assigned us a lovely, three-bedroom villa in Al Sufouh, with a maid's room and four bathrooms (all villas and condos are built with an additional, tiny room that is meant for live-in help… more on that later). Many companies do offer housing but the majority will give a housing allowance. Make sure that it is included as part of the compensation package and do your homework to get a feel for what the rents are to ensure that the allowance is sufficient.

"If possible make your company sort out the first place and wait till you get here to choose a more permanent home. Dubai is a huge sprawling city and you'll want to experience it first to get an idea of where you want to live. Rents are very high compared to the UK but you can negotiate," says Susan Castle from Scotland, a success coach and owner of *Outwith the Dots*.

Yes, rents in Dubai are high. There's no way around it but there are some deals to be had if you dig around a bit. Rents have certainly come down a lot since the bubble burst in 2009 but, relatively speaking, it's still expensive if you want to live in a nice neighbourhood, and there are plenty to choose from.

It's common practice to be asked to fork out one year's rent in advance. Some landlords are relaxing this requirement somewhat by accepting two payments instead of one and there have been instances I've heard where you can sign a six-month agreement, but it's still typical to have to pay 100% up front. So, make sure your company is ready to pay your living allowance for the year in one payment upon arrival or when the lease agreement is signed, or have a little nest egg in the bank if you are bankrolling it yourself.

A little side note, if I may… it would be a bad idea to go into debt this early on in your expat experience by taking out a loan. Actually, it's a bad idea to take on much debt at all during your stay in Dubai. If you unexpectedly lose your job (for whatever reason) all your debts will have to be paid before you'll be allowed to leave and you'll only have 30 days once you've been 'terminated'. As always, just weigh the pros and cons and you'll make the best decision based on your current situation.

"Don't over exceed your budget," says Gillian from South Africa. "Rather be conservative with rentals and make sure that you have at least six months salary stashed away for emergencies."

There are places in Dubai that are 'affordable' but I guess it all depends on your budget, doesn't it? And, you have to ask yourself, 'What are my priorities'?

"Budget for at least a month in a cheap, serviced apartment and take time to understand the city before choosing a location to live," says Dave Reeder, a Brit.

So Many Options, So Little Time...

There is a wonderful diversity in types of communities in Dubai. To the south of the city, the rolling hills of The Meadows, Springs (www.meadows-springs.com) and Emirates Hills (www.emirateshill.com) attract families as the villas are big and, in many cases, have good-sized yards. The golf course is a draw too but is usually deserted in mid-summer when the temperatures soar to 45°C or more. It's a great location if you want to be close to the downtown action but far enough away to enjoy quiet family picnics in the numerous parks.

If you prefer 'suburbia' there are sprawling communities east of the city in the desert, like the popular Silicon Oasis (www.siliconoasis.org), Al Warqa and the renowned, environmentally themed, Green Community (www.greencommunity.ae). Just a couple of years ago it felt like they were in the middle of nowhere. Any time a new friend or co-worker who lived 'out there' invited us for dinner it was all I could do to accept graciously and not moan about the long drive we would have to make. It felt longer when all we could see out the windows on both sides for miles and miles were sand dunes and the odd camel to spice things up a bit. The area is much more built up now, especially with the opening of the Dubai Autodrome and Mirdif Town Centre filling in the gaps.

The Dubai Marina (www.dubai-marina.com) and Jumeirah Beach Residence (http://dubaipropertiesgroup.ae/en/properties/Jumeirah-Beach-Residence) tend to attract singles and couples without children, as they are high-rise, multi-purpose, lifestyle complexes. The Palm Jumeirah (www.palmjumeirah.ae) much higher end real estate, attracts well-heeled expats of all ages with a combination of waterfront apartment complexes and humongous villas on 'the fronds' of the man-made, palm tree-shaped island, each with their own private beach. If you like peace and quiet and feeling exclusive but still be a stone's-throw away from the action, it's perfect.

The first time I visited someone on one of the fronds on the leeward side, the silence was almost surreal. It felt like I was in a bubble like Jim Carrey in *The Truman Show*. Serene, yes but I felt like I was suffocating and couldn't wait to get 'ashore'. The windward side (facing towards downtown) with an amazing view of the Burj Al Arab on a clear day is more pleasant in my opinion.

The new 'old town' (www.theoldtown.ae), built around the base of the Burj Khalifa, the *tallest* building in the world, is one of the newest residential areas bordered by the *largest* mall in the world, the Dubai Mall.

Are you getting a feel for the theme of the city? It's wall-to-wall hyperbole. Everything's over the top but it is energising to be a part of it... think New York meets Las Vegas on steroids. Although I'm not a shopper, Dubai Mall was always one of my favourite places to take visitors. There's a mile-long fountain (fashioned after Las Vegas' *Bellagio* fountain) that does a nightly light, sound and water show put to music that takes your breath away. The streams of water sway in time to the music (a mix of Arabic, top 40s and classical) with a crescendo of water cannons that shakes your insides and vibrates your feet. There are several apartment buildings that overlook this spectacle. Wouldn't that be a cool place to live?

Then there are the truly old parts of town like Al Satwa and Karama where you'll find smaller apartments in areas that feel like you're walking down the streets of Mumbai. The smell of curry and cloves wafts through the streets, emanating from apartment windows and Indian restaurants on every corner. I find that enticing because I love Indian food (it's my second favourite after Thai). However, if it's not your thing, it could have a more unpleasant impact on your olfactory senses.

On either side of the creek are Bur Dubai (where you'll find the textile souk) and Deira (where the oldest school in Dubai was built in 1912). If you like older neighbourhoods and want to be close to the airport, either of these areas or even Al Garhoud, might be a good option for you.

Smack dab in between old and new, sandwiched between the main arteries of Sheikh Zayed Road and Jumeirah Beach Road, you can find some real gems in communities like Umm Sequim and Jumeirah.

So you best sit down and outline your preferences to be able to provide them to the agent helping you find your new home. Your company will hopefully have one available to you as part of the relocation package but, if you wind up house hunting on your own, check out www.propertyfinder.ae. There are those who are left to their own devices either because there's no relocation assistance or they choose to go it alone.

"We used *Crowne Relocation* company (www.crownrelo.com). They assigned a lady who helped me in a lot of ways; finding an apartment, furniture shopping, setting up *Etisalat* and DEWA, to registering a doctor for my baby's delivery. She also provided literature such as *Connector* (a magazine) and *Dubai Explorer*," says Zenubia from Pakistan.

A great place to start connecting online is to post questions on expat blogs and websites like the expat forum on <u>www.expatechodubai.com</u>. Local networking group, *Expat Woman*, has a website, <u>www.expatwoman.com</u>, that has a section that regularly posts around 15,000 listings on properties for rent and sale, in partnership with *Property Finder*.

Many newcomers launch out on their own (some with the help of an agent) and armed with plenty of prior research. "I found our apartment on my own using several different real estate agents," says Pam Rollings, American blogger from Pittsburg, PA.

"We were put up in a hotel apartment for one month while we secured an apartment. We found the apartment ourselves – thank goodness for *Dubizzle*," said Helen from the UK.

Dubizzle is a popular source for all things classified, including apartments or homes to rent or buy.

"I was initially put up in serviced apartments for two months. During this time I spoke to others who I was working with for ideas about areas to live in and property contacts. *Dubizzle* was a great resource for me as I have found all property agents here to be very difficult to work with," said Karen Beggs from Northern Ireland.

As with any profession, there are good brokers and agents and bad brokers and agents. If you choose to go this route, try to get a referral.

"When we came on a visit to Dubai we met an estate agent and we managed to get a house through this agent. We did this all ourselves with no assistance from a relocation company," says Georgie Hearson, wife, mother and co-founder of *Heels & Deals*.

"We researched the cost of living, housing and availability of resources. In 2001, these were pretty much non-existent, so it was a big challenge. Housing agents just wanted to sell us what they had, not what we wanted. Finally, we located what we believed to be the ideal location for our needs in Jebel Ali," said Indian expat Shridhar Sampath.

If you do it on your own be cautious. The tenant/landlord laws change from one day to the next, which is typical in Dubai. For the latest rules and regulations where you can check to make sure your rental agreement is fair go to the Real Estate Regulatory Agency (RERA) at www.rpdubai. ae. A registered broker will have access to download a copy of the standard tenancy contract – you won't – but at least you'll know the latest laws. If you have a disagreement with your landlord this is also where you would lodge a complaint with the Rent Committee.

Some advice for any of you moving to Dubai solo: "If you're single, shared accommodation in a villa or large apartment is an option. Get the word out among your work colleagues and friends," says Eithne Treanor, media trainer and conference moderator, *E. Treanor Media,* originally from Ireland. "Otherwise, look at an apartment hotel and see how you might arrange payment. Try not to get stuck on a year's rent in advance."

There's a new website (as of the writing of this book) called www.i-dar.net that tracks rents in all areas of Dubai by pulling statistics from the classifieds (rent is shown in the UAE currency called dirhams). It's a good place to start to review what the range of rentals looks like.

As with opening a bank account, and actually in order to do anything in Dubai, you'll need more copies of your passport and residency permit.

The Practicalities

Here's what you need:

- Dubai bank account (good thing that was *Chapter 2*).

- Copies of passport and residence permit.

- A statement of income (salary certificate) from your employer.

- A security deposit (typically equal to four weeks rent and refundable if the property is left in good condition).

The Five-Step Recap

Step 1

Research going rates for rentals.

Step 2

Negotiate accommodation allowance with your employer.

Step 3

Make list of requirements for the type of community you want.

Step 4

Line up an agent in advance (who will ensure properties are all registered with RERA and submit your lease agreement to the Land Department, which is legally required).

Step 5

Negotiate lease agreement/connect water and electricity (more on this later).

Tip

Hire a registered agent (in advance of your arrival if possible… but get one on referral, unless your company has one they use). The money you'd save doing it yourself isn't usually worth the hassle.

Case Study #1

"The company provided us with accommodation upon arrival. It was a secure, well-equipped, and relatively new apartment in a tower surrounded by a construction zone. However, we had no opening windows and couldn't BBQ or walk our dog anywhere pleasant. After two years, we opted out of company-provided accommodation in favour of a housing allowance so we could choose our own home. This was a calculated risk as the housing allowance is not adjusted in accordance with rental price fluctuations, and once you opt out you are not allowed back into company-provided accommodation. However, so far it has worked out wonderfully and we feel we have a much higher quality of life in our three bedroom villa surrounded by greenery in a friendly neighbourhood."

Amy from Canada

Case Study #2

"On arrival the company allowed us to stay at a hotel apartment for three weeks after which we had to find a place for ourselves. I went through real estate agents and found one (at that time it was called *Alpha*, not sure if they still exist) and went viewing apartments with them until I found the one that was suitable for us in Bur Dubai. I did not drive at the time and that area was pretty easy to walk around and find taxis. Plus a great deal of facilities and amenities were at an easy reach. It was a shock to us to find the places in Dubai very spacious after moving from London's little apartment and we never realised the amount of furniture that we would end up accumulating."

Dhuha, British/Yemini

The Wrap up

One of the beauties of living in Dubai is there is something for everyone and the type of communities and styles of accommodations are as varied as the hundreds of different cultures represented in the expat community. My older, one-storey villa was the polar opposite to the newer two and three-storey villas with cathedral ceilings that other Emirates Airline employees live in. I'm happy we were assigned where we were. I was much more content in my big, green, bougainvillea-laden back yard rather than a zero lot-line hiding-behind-a-high-cement-wall place any day. Each to his or her own, I always say.

Chapter 5

Buying a Property

It is possible for expatriates to buy property in 'freehold' developments in Dubai. Freehold is where you own the domicile and the land it sits on for as long as you live or until you decide to sell it. There are still some restrictions on what you can do to the exterior (similar to home owner association rules in the US) and there will be a transfer fee when you do sell the property.

Many expats bought up apartments and villas off-plan during the building boom in the early 2000s with promises from developers that the purchase would come with a residence visa. Unfortunately, these developers didn't have the authority to make that kind of promise. In 2009, the government clarified that, as a property owner, you could get a multiple entry visitor visa which had to be renewed every six months at a cost of AED 2,000 and the property must be worth at least AED 1 million. That doesn't appeal much when you realize that the rules could change overnight and then you're stuck with a mortgage and the need to renew your visa several times a year.

If you're considering a property purchase as a way to secure residence, there is a new law being contemplated to allow this (2011) but it involves setting up a company in Dubai that would ultimately 'own' the property and then your residence visa would be under the company name.

A *Gulf News* article on June 10, 2011 reported that the Dubai government was considering a new residence visa system for property owners.

"Residence related to property was a main catalyst for buying and selling in the real estate sector especially since the boom. We think this [law] will restore some activity in the market but not like the previous levels in real estate," Tariq Ramadan, chairman of Tharaa Holding was quoted as saying.

The article continued to state, "the costs associated with setting up a company to register the property under it could reach up to AED 40,000 a year and this may deter some buyers".

The official said that the new mechanism would have the property owner establish a company in the free zone with the company owning the property. This would allow the property owner who owns the company to obtain a residence permit on the basis of ownership of the company, not the property.

After this article ran in the *Gulf News* a real estate legal services expert named Taylor Wessing addressed a reader's concern in a regular column called 'Ask the Law: Property Queries' with the following: "Very few of our clients have pursued this option, and your comments reflect the sentiment of many regarding the new regulations. Clearly therefore this is an area that the UAE Government could revisit in an effort to increase the number of investors and thereby provide a much needed boost to the real estate market." The questioner's comments revolved around the exorbitant cost of setting up a company.

A lot of people prefer to put money into something they own rather than throwing it away on rent so, even with some of the downsides to purchasing in Dubai, the buying continues. If you are adamant that you want to buy, it's advisable to have a hefty down payment, as most banks won't loan more than 70% of the value of the property since the 'correction' in 2009.

Just be prepared for a lot of paperwork (but that would be the case no matter where you're buying... when we bought our house in Fort Lauderdale the oodles of papers required seemed endless).

"We bought two apartments in Dubai. We did a lot of research before getting them. The purchasing process wasn't too complicated but a lot of paper work with the banks was required," says Nathalie N from France.

There are plenty of properties available and more coming on the market every day.

According to Jeanette Todd, a Canadian expat (and attorney) who bought an apartment through a real estate agent, it was a "long and protracted process". She suggests, "Use *Better Homes* (www.bhomes.com) or another real estate agent. The postings on *Dubizzle* and some of the other websites may not always be legitimate or have people who actually respond."

She also reminds prospective buyers that local laws apply to real estate so people buying property should get a will done. "This is the website of the lawyer I used and there are some articles there that give you an overview of what can be expected: http://willsuae.com," offered Jeanette.

"I bought an apartment at Dubai Marina. My real estate agent, Marion Abuthina, sorted every step of the process and I can easily say it was the most trouble free experience ever. I was back in the UK for a lot of the time and her ability to manage this transaction was flawless," said Irish expat Eithne Treanor, media trainer and conference moderator with *E. Treanor Media*.

"I would highly recommend Hayley with *Allsop and Allsop,*" said Aussie Debbie Nicol. "She was fantastic to work with when I sold my place but I think she'd be just as wonderful if you were looking to buy."

If you're buying pre-construction, be prepared for delays in completion. It's rare that a development has been completed on the date it was initially meant to be. If you plan to live in the property you purchase, it's probably better to buy one that's already built.

The Practicalities

- You must have a solid job with a company that has been around at least three years.

- You'll need to provide copies of your passport and residence visa (surprise, surprise).

- Have copies of your labour card and/or salary certificate/letter from your company.

- The lender will ask for bank statements for one year to prove a regular income (some will accept six months) as well as a letter from your bank stating you have no out-standing loans.

- Some banks will require that you have life insurance and home insurance before they will give you a mortgage.

The Five-Step Recap

Step 1

Find a good (RERA registered) realtor through word of mouth or recommendation and choose an area you'd like to live (check out www.propertyfinder.ae as a good start to peruse specific areas and available properties).

Step 2

Shop around for the best bank to provide your mortgage (unless you're buying from a developer that only uses a specific bank). Get pre-approval.

Step 3

Once you choose a property your agent will draw up a letter of intent that will be signed by both you and the seller and you'll put down a deposit.

Step 4

Submit all documents to the bank and your mortgage will be processed. This would be a good time to research home insurance too. Often a bank will require verification of insurance before approving a mortgage. Sometimes the insurance is even part of the package in the first year.

Step 5

Transfer ownership at the Dubai Land Department and register the property in your name with RERA (check hours of operation on the website. It's usually 7:30 am to 2:30 pm). Both buyer and seller must be in attendance as this is when the payment is made to the seller.

Tip

On-going updates on property laws in the UAE can be found in *Al Nisr's Property Magazine* (http://gulfnews.com/about-gulf-news/al-nisr-portfolio/property) or on the RERA website at www.rpdubai.ae.

Case Study #1

"We did buy a house to live in before the economic downturn. The main challenge at the time was finding suitable properties because the market was almost at its peak at the time and properties were being snapped up at a crazy rate. The purchasing process went okay but it certainly wasn't as straight forward as buying a property back in the UK."

Claire Fenner, co-founder of *Heels & Deals*

Case Study #2

"We could have lost our deposit due to the bank delays, but the seller was patient. The bank also unilaterally increased the mortgage rate contrary to the documentation and there were a group of 60 disgruntled customers who met and wanted to sue (there were several lawyers who were customers as well and they led the fight). There is no class action here so it would have to be individual law suits and since the CEO was on the parliamentary committee and from a prominent family, I realized legal principles would not trump *wasta* (influence) and did not waste my time and energy on such a suit, but borrowed money from my mom's line of credit. The lawsuits went nowhere to my knowledge. Of course, even closing the mortgage took forever; many emails and calls following up (as people had no idea what to do in such a situation), going to Outsource Zone, www.doz.ae (near Silicone Oasis which took 45 minutes without traffic) only to find that they spelled my name wrong and only after getting angry, sending frustrated emails that we would not go all the way back there again and demanding them to bring it to us, did they, after several weeks delay, bring it to Media City."

(Anonymous expat)

The Wrap up

In my humble opinion, you want to think long and hard before buying a property in Dubai. Certainly don't buy it for an investment as the real estate market, as I understand it, is pretty flat. According to a *Canadian Broadcasting Corporation (CBC)* news report on June 9, 2011, 'Global real estate market cooling' that quoted a Bank of Nova Scotia report, real estate markets throughout the developing world "are losing steam and in some cases, starting to revert into negative territory". If you have 'disposable' income, you're in Dubai for the long haul and you'd prefer not to pour your money into a rental that you don't own, maybe it's an option. If not, I'd stick to the rental, especially if your company is providing a housing allowance that covers it.

Chapter 6

Water, Electricity (DEWA), Gas... and Mail Delivery

I walked into the house and switched on the lights... next chapter!

Oh, right. Not everyone is spoiled like us with a company that literally takes care of *everything*. I count my blessings when I hear some of the horror stories others have gone through to accomplish the simplest tasks. Admittedly, there were a few bumps along the way however, I didn't even know there was such a thing as DEWA (Dubai Electricity and Water Authority) for the first year we were in Dubai. Your DEWA bill is one monthly payment that covers electricity, water, sewage fees and housing fees.

In our accommodation handbook under the Water, Electricity and Sewage section it simply read, "The Company bears the cost of water and electricity consumption of the villa. The bills pertaining to the villa are received directly by the Company and paid by the Accounts Payable Department". Yes!

I realize not everyone is that lucky so if you're managing utilities yourself you should give DEWA a look see at http://www.dewa.gov.ae/default.aspx so you know the drill before you move in. You'll be running the air conditioning practically year round so keep that in mind when you're checking places out and ask what the average DEWA bill is each month. The other issue that newcomers often don't factor in is the cost of lawn watering. If you wind up in a villa that has a nice yard it takes lots of water to keep it green. Most compounds closer to town have no yards so it's not a worry but if you have a family (and/or pets) a yard is probably high on the priority list.

I mentioned that I heard about DEWA only after being in Dubai a year. That was when there was an over consumption issue. The company was looking for ways to cut costs so they put everyone on notice to be more conservative in their water and electricity use. They put a cap on it and monitored for the next year. I'm happy to say that we never exceeded the cap.

Your DEWA bill will include a 'housing fee' for expats. On the *Expat Echo* website (www.expatechodubai.com) it states "Housing fees for expat tenants is calculated on 5% of the unit's annual rent". It goes on to explain that "DEWA is requiring expats both living in freehold (owned) and non-freehold properties to register their accommodation details on the municipality's portal in order to assist them to calculate the associated housing fee and to enable the invoicing of DEWA's monthly utility bills".

If you don't register your details and you've negotiated a lower rent than DEWA has on record, they will bill you based on the rent figures they have in the system.

"Dealing with DEWA is time consuming and difficult," says Aussie expat Kara Boden. "There is always additional documentation required that you didn't know about and don't have on you!"

UK expat Helen had a totally different experience. "We organised everything ourselves. You just need to allow a day to do each thing (water, gas, electricity, phone). Nothing is quick here, but once it's done, it's done! DEWA can now be set up online, which is a great service." I think Helen arrived long after Kara and the services have become a little more streamlined but experiences do continue to vary from person to person depending on the particular situation.

"It was very time-consuming as I was not able to do it on my own as they required my husband to do it all since the bills were in his name," said Dhuha a British/Yemeni expat. "So the first few Saturdays we had were spent on bureaucracies."

If you're using a relocation company, your agent or broker will often be able to assist you with this.

"We got help from our real estate agent getting the utilities set up but the billing for some of this is sporadic and confusing," said American expat and blogger Pam Rolling. "Most of these we have to pay in person since we can't use our US credit cards to pay the bills online."

There is an online application process to initiate your service but in some cases it takes less time to go in person.

"I tried to do this online (https://e-services.dewa.gov.ae) but nothing ever happened," said Alba Micheli Geddes from Italy. "I went in person to their counter and asked nicely to be connected and it took 24 hours."

"It was a pain at first," said fellow Italian expat Ed Capaldi. "But no different than anywhere else in the world."

The Practicalities (for Water and Electricity)

When you file the documentation you'll need to have:

- The most recent DEWA bill (from the landlord).

- A copy of your passport and residence permit.

- The new tenancy contract.

- A UAE credit card if you apply online for activation (you've done that already in *Chapter 2*, right?).

- You may need a salary letter from your employer, but check ahead of time to verify. The tenancy agreement may be sufficient, as you'll have already proven your ability to pay the rent.

At this point, it might be helpful to have a look at the DEWA Customer Guide – http://www.dewa.gov.ae/consumers/customerguide/default.aspx and take it from there.

The Five-Step Recap

Step 1

Gather all the necessary documentation.

Step 2

Find the unique consumer account number that is assigned to the premises (it's a nine digit number that should be on your tenancy agreement or on a number plate near the metre). I actually found ours on the outside of the front door frame.

Step 3

Fill out the DEWA application online (https://e-services. dewa.gov.ae/activation/activationrequest.aspx) but realize that at some point you may have to go into a DEWA office in person.

Step 4

Pay online with a UAE credit card (or at the closest DEWA office).

Step 5

Wait 24 hours (hopefully) and switch on the lights!

Tip

"There's one office of DEWA that seems less busy than the others. It's beyond Mazaya Centre, on the road that runs down the side of Al Wasl."

Debbie Nicol, Australian, creator of *embers of the world* and managing director of *business en motion*.

Case Study #1

"The simplest of things can cause the biggest frustration. Getting connected to electricity, water, TV and Internet can take forever. In a western country you would probably do everything online, here you have to fill in endless paperwork and you will really never know if you have done it correctly. If you had forgotten to fill in the smallest detail, they will just not connect you and never let you know. Traffic is also very intimidating to start with, there is no room for niceties on the road, you have to get your super confidence out and think you are the king/queen of the road. It does help if you have a land cruiser as opposed to a Yaris as well!"

Alba Micheli Geddes, Italian

Case Study #2

"I had to go to the DEWA office myself and going to any government department you will need half a day. When you go to the DEWA office, you have to take a number but it still seems there is no queue process. They have actually opened a coffee stall there because that's how long you can expect to be there! Whilst waiting, an Arab man called me over to process my application in front of approximately 20 Indian people. I refused as I find this sort of preferential behaviour completely unacceptable."

Karen Beggs, British expat from Northern Ireland

Gas Delivery

Some villas have electric ovens and some have gas stoves and there are companies that will deliver the gas tanks to your door. When we moved in to Flamingo Villas, the accommodation handbook had a list of numbers for us to call for various services. The gas company they recommended and that we used was *Laheej Gas Distributors* (no website but the office number is 04 337 6686). *Emirates Gas* has several distributors that do home delivery as well (www.emiratesgas.ae).

When we called to have the cylinder filled we also asked them to put on a dual nozzle so the same tank could be hooked up to the stove and the barbeque at the same time. Our neighbour had complained that he had to keep switching it every time he wanted to barbeque or buy two tanks. My brilliant husband knew there was a way to put a splitter on the tank and convinced *Laheej* to put one on for us. Halas! That's Arab for 'finished'. I use that word a lot since moving to the Middle East.

There's no recap or wrap up and just one step. If you need propane, choose the company and make the call.

Mail Delivery

There is no home delivery of mail in the UAE. All mail is sent to a central postal station and then distributed to various PO Boxes throughout the Emirates. You can either set up a personal PO Box at one of the branches (hopefully there's one close to where you live) or have mail sent to your company's address.

For some, this is a jarring realisation. "I had no idea you needed a PO Box and so didn't receive any birthday cards," says Dawn from Ireland.

There is an online registration form to rent a personal PO Box at www.emiratespostuae.com. You will need to pay for a pick up and delivery service or bring the form personally into a physical branch with:

- Passport copies with residence permit and

- Passport photos

For an updated list of post office branches visit <u>www.</u> <u>dubaifaqs.com/post-offices-dubai.php.</u>

The Wrap up

Online services with all Dubai government departments are in the early stages of development. Some work well and others are works in progress. My suggestion is that you give the online interface a try initially (since we *are* in the 21st century) and give it a day or two to be confirmed. Chances are, you'll be successful. If it doesn't work, be prepared to go in person rather than have a customer service representative help you over the phone. In most cases, they have minimal training and wind up asking you to come in to the service centre anyways. Just look at it as a great way to get some driving practice in and get to know your way around a little better. A little hint... start noticing landmarks because that's the way people in Dubai give directions. So, get into the habit of taking in your surroundings differently than you're used to and take note of that huge flag, for example, at the end of Jumeirah Beach road almost to the creek. At some point, someone is bound to tell you that something is near the 'big flag'.

Chapter 7

Landline and Broadband Services – Connecting your Lifelines

The Landline (AKA your 'Home Phone')

Amazingly enough in the 21st century, and as forward thinking and cosmopolitan as the UAE is, again be prepared to head in person to an actual physical office with all your documentation to complete your application for a landline (if you're not lucky enough to already have one in your villa or apartment as we did).

It's advisable to purchase a mobile phone with a pay as you go SIM card right away so you have a way to communicate while you go through the process of getting your landline set up. *Chapter 17* goes more into mobile phones and SIM cards.

Definitely start doing the research online before you arrive. The two providers are *Etisalat* (www.etisalat.ae) and *du* (www.du.ae). Compare and contrast packages and then make your choice. However, many communities and apartment buildings are already wired through one or the other. Our compound uses *Etisalat*. Having the choice made for you does save a lot of time and hassle as long as you're not a control freak and hate being told what to do.

"We live in The Springs so we have to stick to *du*," says Lebanese expat Rawan Albina. "The process was quite efficient and fast."

So, there's the good news. If you already have a landline installed in your home (as Rawan and I did), in theory, you should be able to do this over the phone (using the pay as you go mobile, or a friend's since you won't have phone service yet). Give it a try but always be prepared to go in person to complete the transaction. Sometimes it just depends on whom you talk to. It's a cultural thing. Emiratis are used to doing business face-to-face. As much as they are embracing new technological advancements, they just love to see our smiling faces.

If you do have to go to one of the business centres, it will be a lengthy wait so don't plan to go back to work. If you're thinking you can do it over your lunch break just put that thought right out of your head. Bring a magazine (or two) or a good book. I recommend something funny like Erma Bombeck or even a Calvin and Hobbs, as you'll need to maintain your sense of humour and continue smiling no matter what happens. Remember, no amount of foot stomping or huffing and puffing will do you any good. It will actually make things worse for you and you'll probably be labelled what Maria Foley @Iwasanexpatwife calls 'an ugly expat'. She did a great guest blog on <u>www.</u> <u>expatica.com</u> called 'Become an ugly expat in 12 easy steps'. Don't do it...

There's some good advice. Keep smiling and it will get you much further than if you raise your voice and make demands. Your *friendly* customer service representative will most likely shut down if you do. Or worse, accuse you of being disrespectful and possibly report you to the police. Yes, they can do that and some actually will.

Too Many Zeros...

A little side note... initially, you're more than likely to puzzle over the 'to dial zero or not to dial zero' conundrum. When someone gives you their telephone number note if it starts with 050 or 04. A 050 number (or 055 or 056) indicates a mobile phone and 04 is a landline in Dubai. Each Emirate has a distinct landline code. Abu Dhabi is 02, for example. If you call landline to landline, you don't have to dial the 04. If you're calling from a mobile, you will.

If you're giving your number to a friend or relative who will be calling long distance (there are those, like my mother, who don't have *Skype*) they will have to add an international code (like 011), the country code (971) and then drop the first 0. So it would be +971 4 555 2222, for a landline and +971 50 222 5555 for a mobile, for example.

Speaking of *Skype*, when we first moved to Dubai it was blocked. People found various and assorted ways of bypassing this through VPNs (virtual private networks) and such but there seems to be an easing up on that lately. *Skype* access, however, is still variable. Last I checked, you still couldn't download any updates but you could sometimes get through on the regular Internet portals.

Once you have a landline set up, you can get a calling card that is linked to your home phone (for post-paid plans only). If you travel a lot it's not a bad idea. There is no additional charge to get the card and when you use it the fee is just added to your monthly bill.

Broadband – Getting on 'The Net'

Now that you have your landline sorted out you can easily (I say this tongue in cheek) add your Internet package. The prerequisite is to have any account in your name (either a landline or mobile) and you should be able to accomplish this online as long as you've set up an Internet login.

"The Internet is a must and with it you can do Internet video conferencing such as *Skype*, Instant Messenger (*MSN*) or *Google* Talk. We also plug a *magicJack* (www. magicjack.com) into the computer for $20 a year with free calls to the US and an American phone number for others to call," says W Mervis, an American expat. "My husband likes *Web Phone* (www.webphone.com) to call phones everywhere else."

Internet 'pipelines' throughout the UAE vary greatly from community to community. Some of the newer developments have high-speed access and some, like ours, didn't. We lived in an older neighbourhood that I loved because there were lots of trees, birds chirping and children playing and it had a generally lived in feel to it. It wasn't so charming though when the Internet kicked off or a simple download took half an hour. But, we were reassured that the fibre that would enable a faster connection had been laid and the upgraded services would be available sometime before the end of the year... and so, the community waits.

I try not to complain too loudly to my other expat compatriots living in less developed parts of the world who tromp down donkey paths to the one Internet café in town in the hopes of hopping on a computer that may or may not be working that day. Or, like *Bitten by Spain* author, Debbie Fletcher, who lives in a caravan in a valley in a remote, rural area of Spain with no signal whatsoever. Okay, today's reality check is complete.

"We use *du* for our apartment (the only option) and the service has been fine for Internet, cable TV and local phone. It's cheaper if you get all three, even though we don't need the landline," said American expat and blogger, Pam Rollings.

For mobile broadband services (for Internet access from your mobile phone for example) of course you'll be charged not by the minute but by the gigabyte (GB) in data packages. Read the plan carefully and understand what constitutes a GB, which are often broken down into the smaller denomination of Megabytes (MB). My friends who use this tell me that you can eat through the little devils pretty fast. *Etisalat* offers one, five and 10 GB packages that cost AED 145, AED 295 and AED 395 respectively.

You should be able to find updated information on mobile data usage plans at www.etisalat.ae/online or www.du.ae/en/mobile/mobilebroadband.

No Need to be Tied to your Desk

If you like to move around the house with laptop in tow, wireless modems can be purchased. We've been a wireless family for years now and we did get a wireless modem router from *Etisalat* that we used quite happily. It did need to be reset fairly frequently (the same goes for the wired variety), especially on the weekends, but as long as I know where the button is, I'm happy.

The Practicalities

- Application forms for both *Etisalat* and *du* can be downloaded from their websites and will save a little time for when you go in person.

- Passport copies including residence visa page (of course, I've heard from some people that you could be asked to see the original).

- Tenancy agreement and/or utility bill (bring both just in case).

- Salary letter from your employer.

- The Dubai regional office telephone number for *Etisalat* is +971 4 222 8111.

- The *du* main office customer service number is +971 4 360 0000.

The Five-Step Recap

Step 1

Review and compare details of *Etisalat* and *du* plans and choose one (unless you don't have an option as the community or compound has already committed to one or the other).

Step 2

Get copy of tenancy contract (lease agreement).

Step 3

Gather all appropriate documentation and download online application.

Step 4

Go to *du* or *Etisalat* business centre with application and documentation.

Step 5

Wait patiently.

Tip

Cable TV packages can be organised through your telecommunications provider (*Etisalat* or *du*) and will come through *E-Vision* (*Etisalat* only), *Showtime*, *Orbit* or *ART*.

Case Study #1

"I have used both *du* and *Etisalat*. If you live in a relatively well-established area of town, you're okay. Although, they expect you to stay home for eight-hour stretches waiting for them to arrive for installations, etc. Be firm and give them a four-hour window and your mobile number. If you live somewhere quite new, heaven help you."

Amy from Canada

Case Study #2

"*du* is my Internet provider. It was relatively easy and quite good at giving you a time for a visit and sticking to it. Both *du* and *Etisalat* let themselves down with their customer care… dreadful! They have standard phrases that they have been taught but they have never been taught to think things through and therefore at the end of their detailed reasoning as to why something isn't working it's "sorry ma'am, I don't know". Trying to find a line manager is like looking for a needle in the proverbial haystack. *du's* new office on Sheikh Zayed Road does seem to work efficiently. However, to retrieve the AED 2,000 deposit for international roaming took numerous phone calls and a visit to their offices where the assistant took at least 20 minutes to finalise the paperwork through their computer system."

Fiona Thomas, marketing specialist from Scotland

The Wrap up

At this point you probably need a break from the bureaucracy and red tape of getting your life set up in Dubai. Time for a little exploration maybe? A couple of places to connect to early on, especially if you're a do-it-your-selfer, are the Al Karama (it actually has a *Facebook* page) and Al Satwa areas. Not only are there great, ethnic restaurants but rows and rows of little shops selling everything from nuts and bolts to bolts of fabric. It's a great place to find the extra cabling you may need to get your phones, computers and modems connected or even an extra phone or two. You'll definitely find better deals than if you went to the one and only good sized hardware store in town, *Ace Hardware* (although we did buy our back yard furniture there). Note… the only commonality between Ace Hardware in Dubai and the well-known brand in the US, is the logo. I'm not Mrs Fixit by any stretch of the imagination but according to my husband, the staff has no product knowledge and the managers don't seem to care. There is actually another smaller hardware store in Al Quoz beside the Oasis Centre called Speedex that's slightly more reasonable than ACE but I'd still check out Al Karama and Al Satwa. Just make a note that most of the shops in these areas close from around 1 pm to 4 pm.

Chapter 8

Help in and Around the House

I've never seen a place before where everyone (and I do mean *everyone*) has help inside and outside of the house… because, you can… and, it's cheap… and, it's right on your doorstep! Literally.

It started the day we moved in. Well, actually the first knock on the door was my neighbour Wendy, from across the street, with a bottle of wine in hand. I welcomed her with open arms and she's become a close friend. She would have become a close friend with or without the wine but it was a nice touch.

So, let's go back to the doorstep. In some communities in the US there's a program called 'Welcome Wagon' where you're contacted when you move in (it's usually connected to a real estate company) and you're given little gifts and tons of coupons from vendors and service providers in the local area. What descended upon us that first week was more like a disorganised 'chuck wagon' dropping dribs and drabs of various and assorted vendors along the street, who arrived at our front door, offering their services. The knock on the door that followed Wendy's was Ahmed. He was a gardener who did work for other villas in the compound and wanted to know if we needed a gardener.

"Do we need a gardener?" I called over my shoulder to Doug as I smiled uncertainly at Ahmed. I didn't know.

"Actually, we're definitely going to need help with the landscaping," he called back. "Ask him how much he charges."

I hadn't thought of that. We did need a machete to get through the overgrown hedge to get into our front gate. And, the back yard was a disaster. This was one of the few things the company didn't take care of.

So, Ahmed was the first 'helper' we hired but he certainly wasn't the last. That same week we had maids, carpenters, electricians, curtain-makers, painters and plumbers knocking on the door. I barely had to pick up the phone before the tradesman I needed knocked on the door. I almost jumped at the first offer of a maid but then realised that it would be hard to justify since I wasn't working (yet) and didn't have any kids. The two of us plus a cat don't make a whole lot of mess. It's a good thing I said no because, at the time, what I didn't know was that it would have been illegal for me to hire that lovely, smiling girl who knocked on my door. Maids must be sponsored full-time as live-in help or you have to hire from companies like *Molly Maid* (www.mollymaidme.com). You can't just use someone else's maid part-time even if the sponsoring family says it's okay. But, you can get someone once or twice a week through a licensed company.

"I don't have a full time maid, just a maid service on a Sunday morning for four hours. The company is *Dial-A-Maid* (http://dubaimaids.ae) and they are run by a Western lady. They are great," says Helen from the UK.

Those who need more than a little help opt to hire and sponsor a full-time, live-in maid. The majority of maids in Dubai hail from India, Sri Lanka, Philippines, Ethiopia, Bangladesh, and Indonesia. These are the pre-approved countries from where the Dubai government will allow maid visas. I have no idea why but that's the rule.

Of course, there are exceptions to every rule... even in Dubai. One of my neighbours is from Kenya and wanted to hire a maid from there as she had friends who could help with a referral. If you hire a maid from your home country, you will need to prove that you are not related. She was keen on having someone whose language she could speak a little (in this case, Swahili) and was willing to go through the extra step since the referral was a good one.

Most people who have been through the process will strongly urge that you find a maid through a referral.

"We have a full-time live-in helper and without her support our family could not operate in the way it does! We found her through a friend who knew her previous employer. The process was fairly smooth as she was already a UAE resident and my husband's company helped process the paperwork required for her visa and labour contract," said Claire Fenner, co-founder of *Heels & Deals*.

I may have mentioned before that all accommodations (even most apartments) have a room specifically for 'the maid'. They're always close to the kitchen and laundry room (and can often be closed off from the rest of the house) and they're usually pretty small. The maids I've talked seem to be pretty content to have their own space though, no matter how small. Since we don't have a maid, we use ours for storage.

"It's such a common practice to have a live-in housekeeper that it's literally built into the infrastructure of the houses. Most houses have 'maid's quarters' which essentially consists of a very small room and bathroom. I had initially envisioned maid's quarters to be a detached little house on a sprawling estate, not a tiny room inside a four-bedroom house. I lived in our house for weeks before I even knew what our 'extra little room' was for. Now we use it as a place to iron; it's roughly eight feet by six feet," comments American expat Lynda Skok Martinez on her blog *Longhorns and Camels*, http://longhornsandcamels. wordpress.com.

Finding Your Lifesaver

There are a variety of ways to find and secure your live-in help. It's always easier if she's already in the UAE and is being referred by another family who may be leaving Dubai and helping her find a new assignment.

"She is a gift from god and we call her 'mother Mary'," says Australian Sarah Walton who blogs as *The Hedonista* at www.thehedonista.com. "I found her through expatwoman.com, where her temporary employer (also Australian) had placed an ad for her. I met her in an interview, and had no idea what to ask her, so just offered her the job and asked how much I should pay her. Everything was easy from then on."

Or, you might choose to go through an agency.

"The process in hiring her was very efficient. You need to find the right agency. I had called the Philippine embassy at the time and asked them which agency they recommend and that's how I got through to *Allujain Agency*," said Rawan Albina, wife, mother and professional certified coach from Lebanon.

"We decided we needed one (a live-in helper) once our son was born. A friend of hers who worked in Dubai recommended her, after direct hire from an agency catalogue proved disastrous," said British/Yemeni expat Dhuha. "I asked an agency to do the whole procedure of bringing her into the country with a working visit visa and then we had to apply for her residency within two months of arrival which my husband's company did for us so it was not as painful, but quite expensive."

Once you've found her, keeping her happy is important too as it's a process you don't want to be going through over and over again.

"I have a nanny and it was pretty easy to find her as I had a very clear idea of what my needs were. Plus we live in an area where her extended relatives live, so that's an added incentive and happiness factor," says Marissa Woods, British expat, personal brand expert and entrepreneur. "I know so many people where the nanny is not happy and it affects the child and the family. Always be so careful about referrals and recommendations, just as if you were hiring for a full-time workplace job. Treat it the same way… your child deserves it!"

Everyone wants to be appreciated. I know when I was teaching preschool I took my role as caregiver and teacher very seriously and it made me feel good when parents recognised how important (and sometimes difficult) that role can be.

A Few Recommendations

Expatforum.com included the following when a visitor asked about maid service in Dubai (I only included ones I could find a website address for):

- *Howdra* - www.howdra.ae

- *Focus Cleaning* - www.focusmaids.com/contactus.html

- *Ready Maids* - www.readymaidsdubai.com

- *Right Maids* - www.rightmaids.net

- *Solutions Hygiene* - www.solutionshygiene.com

- *Home Maid* - www.homemaids.ae

Many of the other companies listed were part of the *Dial-a-Maid* network.

Here again are the website addresses for those mentioned earlier:

- *Molly Maid* - www.mollymaidme.com

- *Dial-a-Maid* - http://dubaimaids.ae

Paying Your Live-in Help

According to the Dubai Government, the minimum salary ranges from AED 750 to AED 1,400 per month, depending on the minimum wage laws of your maid's country of origin. The sponsor is obligated to provide room and board, one day a week off, plus paid home leave for about a month once every two years.

A friend of mine employs a maid from Sri Lanka, and they are required to pay her a minimum salary of AED 825 a month. They choose to pay more as they feel it's only fair and they want her to stay with them. She's become part of the family. One year, on renewal of her visa, the immigration officer asked why she was being paid so much when my friend could hire a maid from Bangladesh for AED 750. My friend was flabbergasted and just mumbled some sort of excuse, signed the renewal paperwork and left.

The Practicalities

The official portal of the Dubai Government (www.dubai. ae) lists the following criteria for sponsorship of a full-time, live in maid/nanny:

Documents Required for Maid Residence Visa:

- Salary certificate of sponsor in Arabic or labour contract of sponsor.

- Accommodation contract showing minimum two-bedroom apartment.

- Typed application form from authorized typing office.

- Copy of sponsor's passport and visa of the head of the household whose salary is not less than AED 6,000 a month or AED 5,000 plus accommodation. Note: Bachelors are not eligible to sponsor a maid.

- Copy of maid's passport.

- Passport photos of maid (minimum three required).

- Affidavit from embassy/consulate certifying non-relationship, if maid is from same country as sponsor.

- Blood test, chest x-ray and tuberculosis test results.

The Five-Step Recap

Step 1

Decide whether you want or need a full-time live-in helper or if you can manage with someone coming just a couple days a week.

Step 2

If you only need part-time, call one of the services listed and book an appointment. If you want a full-time, live-in maid, start the process by either contacting an agency to walk you through the process or by making the inquiries online and among friends for a recommendation.

Step 3

Once you've found someone you'd like to hire, go to an authorized typing centre to get the appropriate form filled out (either you or the agency you've hired will do this).

Step 4

Go to the General Directorate of Residency and Foreigners Affairs in Bur Dubai and submit all documents. You can pay an extra fee and have the employment entry permit approved on the same day (for which you pay a refundable fee of AED 2,000). Send a copy to your maid and file the original at DNATA Visa Desk at Dubai airport or at a DNRD counter.

Step 5

Once she enters the county with her work permit, you then get a medical fitness report (you may have to pick it up or the clinic will forward it to DNRD, depending on where you go). Then you can apply for her residence visa at any DNRD branch (again, forms can be collected at an authorized typing centre). Go to residency section of DNRD and submit residency visa typed application with employment entry permit and all other required documentation. Bring your maid with you to save time. A residence stamp valid for one year will be placed in her passport and she will get a Domestic Worker Identity Card. This must be done within 30 days of her arrival.

> **Tip**
> With the transient nature of Dubai's huge expat community, families move constantly and often try to find good placements for their maids or nannies, some who have become 'just like family'. Check online forums and notice boards outside grocery stores like Spinneys, Choithrams and Park 'n' Shop for leads.

Case Study #1

"We have a full time maid/nanny. The first one we had, we had to let go. She was apparently 'persona non grata' in Dubai. We found that out when we applied for her visa. Now we have a new maid with whom we're very happy. The first maid was recommended to us and just showed us you can't trust anybody. Sad, but true. The second one we posted for online via *Expat Woman*. We had a number of replies, a few interviews and made a choice, deciding to give our new maid the benefit of the doubt. And we're happy to say we made the right choice."

Vibeke Nurgberg, Denmark

Case Study #2

"The process is similar to getting a residence visa for yourself. Take her for blood tests and medical certificate, bring three photographs. Collect Medical Certificate. Take her passport, medical certificate and photographs to Immigration (I use the Bin Sougat location). Include a letter from sponsor's employer confirming that sponsor does work for company. Get application typed and translated. Pay money. Wait in queue to get visa."

Pam Wilson, British, (grew up in Zimbabwe), managing director of *Silla*

The Wrap up

My friends and neighbours who have live-in nannies and maids are extremely grateful and, in many cases, treat them like one of the family. I even have one neighbour who provides room and board not only to the maid but to her husband and child as well. However, there are sad stories of maids being abused and they have little recourse. I think it's so important to remember that most of the labourers in Dubai (including maids) have left children behind in their home country and have come to Dubai to make money to send home so their children can live a better life. They're to be commended not treated like slaves.

Chapter 9

Getting a Driving Licence

When I read in a local guidebook that you have to fail your driving test five times before you can complain about your examiner, I laughed so hard I snorted. I remembered my friend Ksenia from Bosnia regaling us with stories of her driving lessons. One day her instructor started yelling at her and asking her why she had stopped.

"Well," said Ksenia uncertainly. "There's a stop sign."

"But there's nothing coming!" yelled the instructor.

If you don't stop at a stop sign where I'm from, and just slow down, that would be called a 'rolling stop' and a hefty fine comes with it. I am certain that if Ksenia didn't stop at a stop sign during her driving test in Dubai, she would probably fail. But, it would be her fault, not the instructors, right? Unbelievable!

If you have a driver's licence from certain countries (for an updated list of exempt countries check out

www.dubaifaqs.com/driving-licence-exchange-uae.php)
or an international driver's licence you will be saved from
the humiliation of being 'taught' how to drive by someone
who is probably one of the worst drivers in the world,
according to Ksenia. All you have to do is present your
valid driver's licence at one of the RTA (www.rta.ae)
branches (along with all the other reams of paperwork),
pay the fee and go along your merry way.

"I do drive in Dubai and getting my driver's licence was
a relatively easy process," says Georgie Hearson, co-
founder of *Heels & Deals*. Georgie is from the UK so
could simply transfer her licence, unlike poor Ksenia. She
also offers some words of caution. "In Dubai, due to the
fact that we spend a lot of time on the roads, particularly
highways, you have to make sure you have your wits about
you more than ever and be prepared that some drivers do
the unexpected!" They're probably jumping stop signs if
they had an instructor like Ksenia's.

The day I went to the Roads and Transport Authority
(RTA) to get my licence was December 24. I remember
it vividly. I had only been in Dubai for nine days and
it was a rare day off for Doug and he drove me there.
We arrived at the Al Barsha location (near Mall of the
Emirates) in plenty of time (they closed at 2:30 pm and
we arrived there at 1 pm). I was automatically sent to the
'typing centre' where most people start, not realising that
I already had everything I needed, thanks to the Emirates
employee assistance centre. They had already taken care
of the Arabic letter I needed. After waiting for my turn for

about half an hour, the nice Emirati gentleman reached for my paperwork, flipped through it, handed it back to me saying, "No need for this". He meant his services. So, back I went to the first room and waited about 45 minutes for someone to call my number. There was no one else in front of me and three women sitting doing nothing behind the counter so, I finally walked up at around 2:15 and asked if they could help me.

"I'm closed, come back tomorrow," was the unhelpful reply.

"But I've been here since one o'clock," I answered politely fighting back the desire to remind her that it was Christmas the next day and I would rather not come back. "And you don't close until 2:30 and it's only 2:15."

"Go to Jumeirah office. They're open until nine tonight." She turned to her friend. I was dismissed.

Fortunately, I was successful in convincing the gentleman at the end of the row (who seemed to be the only one doing any work) to process my paperwork. I had seen from those that went before me that it only took about five minutes if your paperwork was in order. I finally left with my UAE driving licence in hand as they locked the door behind me.

Then the challenge began getting used to the roads in Dubai.

"I drove in Dubai. But it took me months to start to feel confident enough. The traffic is horrible and often you're left with the feeling that other drivers really don't care if you live or die. The signs on roads are often misguiding and it takes time to get to know the city. One wrong turn could mean a re-route of several kilometres... maybe up to 30," said Danish expat Vibeke Nurgberg.

Maybe it's better not to have any prior experience. It's like a baptism by fire.

"I learned to drive in Dubai and got my first ever driver's licence. What an experience! It would just take me too long to explain but I will just say that my first instructor didn't speak English and she had 11 fingers between two hands... I passed the first time on a manual car and I am very proud of myself for that. You really need to be assertive and growl at people or you will be `taken for a ride`," said Alba Micheli Geddes from Italy.

Seems like it's been that way for a long time...

"I got my driving licence in Sharjah 20 years ago. It was one of the most difficult things to get, because back in those days, if you failed a test, you had to wait three months to get another test date. There's been enough written about the dangerous driving here – just drive down Sheikh Zayed Road any time of the day or night, and you'll know what I mean," said long-time Indian expat Padmini Sankar.

108

Actually, it's all relative, and depends on where you come from according to Lebanese expat, Rawan Albina who moved to Dubai from Kuwait. "At the time our Kuwaiti licence was simply exchangeable. I bought my car off *Dubizzle* in 2006. No hassle at all! The roads compared to the roads in Beirut are state of the art and really stress-free. Of course you occasionally get the tail-gaters but nothing is perfect," she said.

If you haven't come from Beirut or another equally driving-challenged country, your experience may be a little more trying.

"I drive in Dubai and let me say that the experience has increased my confidence level in addition to making me feel invincible! Anyone who can successfully navigate the roads and the drivers in Dubai is to be commended! It is one of the scariest and riskiest things I have ever done! I know that if I can drive here, I can drive anywhere," said American Shirley W Ralston.

If you've moved around a lot and have experience driving in several different countries then you're well versed in adapting to new road systems and local driving habits.

"Getting a driver's licence was the easiest and quickest procedure. So was buying (and selling) of our cars. The road network is good but signage is not the best. Having had life experiences in both developing countries (Africa) and developed countries (UK), I'm better prepared and equipped in terms of expectations and skills," says

Bijay Shah, national director, *BNI (Business Networking International*) Middle East.

If you are from one of the non-exempt countries, you need to do classes, lessons and a driver's test, like Ksenia did. I've seen *Belhasa Driving School* or *Emirates Driving Institute* (www.edi-uae.com) all over town but don't have any personal recommendation to offer. I think it's pretty much hit and miss (hopefully not literally).

If you read AA Gill's account of his experience that he wrote about in a *Vanity Fair* article 'Dubai on Empty' in the April 2011 issue, you may decide to never drive in Dubai anyway.

"My driver gets lost more than once. He's lived here all his life. He says he always gets lost. The roads keep changing. It's a confusion of orange traffic cones and interlocking barriers; access roads peter out into long drops to rubble and dust. Nothing actually goes anywhere. The wide lanes loop around endlessly, and then there's no place to go," writes Gill.

I admit, there are days I drive around in circles because the turn I normally take to get somewhere no longer exists but I tell myself it's all in the name of progress. For some updates on road works you can visit www.rta.ae.

Then, there's always the opposing view...

"I have been driving from Al Garhoud to Jumeirah for nine years because my kids go to school that side. I am probably the only one in Dubai who does not think the driving is awful. I sometimes come across inconsiderate drivers but I choose to ignore them and make every effort to get out of their way. The roads are excellent and I find drivers (again my opinion) to be courteous most of the time… and I do a lot of driving," said British expat Pam Wilson, managing director of *Silla*.

The Practicalities

- Original passport and photocopy (including residence visa).

- Original valid driving licence from country of citizenship and photocopy (and translation depending on originating country).

- If you have an un-exchangeable driving licence you will either have to do a road test or take driving lessons.

- Eye test (tell them you need it for your driving licence application).

- You will also most likely require two passport-sized photos. Have you run out yet? You'll need two for the licence application in addition to the ones for the eye test.

- No objection letter from your sponsor (company or spouse).

- Application form in Arabic (can be done at any typing centre... there's one at every RTA location where you will apply for your licence).

- Consulate letter for Canadians (check with the consulate to make sure).

The Five-Step Recap

Step 1

Take lessons and driving test (for non-exempt drivers).

Step 2

Gather all documents (and nerves of steel).

Step 3

Head to the closest Roads and Transport Authority (RTA) Traffic Department office. Remember Al Barsha? It's open 7:30 am to 2:30 pm but the Jumeirah Beach location is open until 9 o'clock at night.

Step 4

Visit the typing office (there's usually one on site), unless your company has taken care of the Arabic letter and application for you. If so, you can skip this step.

Step 5

Submit all relevant documents, take a number and have a seat...

Note: As in most places, a special licence is required to drive a motorcycle.

Tip

"Take your time and never let your guard down. Expect everyone to do something wacky, and then you'll be okay. At the beginning, I was sure I would never be able to do it. Now I sometimes take the fast lane on Sheikh Zayed Road! I don't speed, though and I still try to stop for pedestrians and yield to ambulances, even though this is not the norm here."

Amy, Canadian

Case Study #1

You need eyes in all four corners of your head. Expect the unexpected, realise that there are 100 different nationalities on the roads with 100 different driving styles. Road layouts change every week so you're rarely going where you think you're going. It can be pretty hair-raising. People regularly reverse down motorways if they've missed their turn off and also reverse round roundabouts for the same reason. If there's a bad accident, people will stop and get out to take photographs… yes, in the middle of the motorway. As with most things in Dubai, keep a sense of humour at all times or it will drive you crazy."

Susan Castle, Scottish, owner *Outwith the Dots*

Case Study #2

"You have to keep a sense of humour about the lack of consistency and transparency of rules and regulations. For instance, the 'Roads and Transport Authority' will not disclose over the phone how much it costs to get a driver's licence, because apparently you just find out when you get there. My guidebook printed this year (2011) said it would cost AED 140. It actually cost AED 400. Lesson learned: things like this are quite arbitrary. Seeing something in print doesn't make it so."

Lynda Skok Martinez, blogger, *Longhorns and Camels*

The Wrap Up

Dead-ends and roundabouts aside, during the three and a half years I lived in Dubai, I saw some marked improvement in the road systems. The police are also cracking down on unsafe drivers and they've installed speed cameras along all the major roadways, and claim it has had a positive impact on accidents. Every once in a while there will be a new video on YouTube of young Emiratis screeching down Sheikh Zayed Road on two tires or pulling doughnuts in the middle of Jumeirah Beach Road but it's usually in the wee hours of the morning. As a general rule, I avoided the roads between about 10 pm and dawn.

Chapter 10

Getting from Here to There

If you decide that the license-getting and car-buying processes are just too daunting, there is public transport and inexpensive taxis. However, using them every day can take quite a chunk out of the budget and you just might prefer to be in control of your own destiny.

"I use taxis periodically and find the service excellent although lately I do feel that they have increased their speed and have had to ask drivers to slow down. Something has changed in their lives I think; they seem impatient and not happy. My teenagers use the metro and I have on occasion, it is brilliant," said Pam Wilson, British, managing director of *Silla*.

Public Transport

Taxis

Dubai Taxi (part of the RTA, www.rta.ae) has a pretty streamlined service and once they pick you up at your residence one time, they have it logged in their system. When you call again at 208-0808 from your landline, in just a few button presses, your request is submitted and verified. Taxis can often be easily flagged down on the side of the road (as long as it's not during peak times). There's a minimum charge of AED 10 for most destinations. However, the metre starts at AED 20 as soon as you place your butt in a taxi at the Dubai Airport or at Mina Rashid Port (if you happen to be getting off a cruise ship). Then you'll pay AED 1.60 per km after that.

Buses and Metro

As I've personally weighed the pros and cons, I found the biggest problem with public transport is that the Metro (which only goes north/south along Sheikh Zayed Road) and the buses (which only connect from a few Metro stops to main arteries and not into suburbs) don't seem to connect as well as the systems you may be used to in London or Toronto or any other big city where you may have lived. You may decide that it's an inconvenience you're willing to live with since it's a very cost effective way to travel. You can get from one end of Dubai to the other for less than AED 10. But there are other issues to take into consideration.

"I try to use the Metro system more now but I still have to drive to the nearest station as the bus takes three times the time to get there," says Claire Fenner, co-founder and managing director of *Heels & Deals*. "I use the Metro when I'm going for meetings in town where the parking can be busy but in the hotter months only as long as the building I'm going to is a short distance from the Metro station."

Dubai Metro and Dubai Bus routes, fares and times can be checked on the RTA portal at www.rta.ae or on www.dubaicityinfo.com.

Buying (or Leasing) a Car

So, for most people, a car is a necessity. My friends who don't have cars are always looking for rides or waiting for taxis. It can be a real time waster, especially on the weekends… if the taxi comes at all.

When we first moved to Dubai we leased a car for three months. We used *Sixt* car rental (www.sixt.com) and it was reasonable in comparison to Western standards. That was in 2007 so I'm sure the rates have changed. Don't book online though. They'll hose you. Wait until you get to Dubai, take taxis for a few days and do some research on car rental rates by phone. I've seen rates as low as AED 515 per week. A great place to start your research is www.dubairentalcargroup.com.

After that, we bought two cars, one from *Al Futtaim* (www.alfuttaimmotors.ae) and one in a private sale. Both purchases were pretty painless other than the fact that we rear-ended a lady with our Jeep before we had even transferred the paperwork from the previous owner. One positive outcome was learning how wonderful car insurance companies are... responsive, efficient and helpful.

Car Insurance and Roadside Assistance

We used *AXA Insurance*. There's not much competition so it was a pleasant surprise how wonderful they were. I know of several people who use the same insurance company as us but another option is *Royal Sun Alliance* that the ladies on an Expat Woman forum (www.expatwoman.com/forum) were raving about.

Your insurance company will usually offer emergency roadside assistance, as did the dealership where we bought our car. There are other companies, one that even calls itself *AAA* (not the same as the triple-A of the US) that offer emergency services (http://aaaemirates.com). Another, the *Roadside Auto Assistance Centre* (www.rac.ae), has an annual membership fee of AED 500 that gives you free 24/7 access to the services. I've never used it so can't say how reliable it is but it does sound like a great deal. Again, it seemed to be popular among the ladies on the forum.

If your car needs repairs after an accident, your insurance company will tell you where to bring the car if you want them to cover the cost. Otherwise, you can comb the Al Quoz area as there are auto body and repair shops on every corner. But, a word of warning… as with anywhere else in the world, auto mechanics can be a dodgy bunch. Get a recommendation and watch them like a hawk. Unfortunately, parts are ridiculously expensive so ask for costs upfront so you don't go into sticker shock.

As with most services, it's always best to get a recommendation from a friend or colleague. If you'd like to explore beyond the insurance companies suggested here, check out www.indexuae.com/Top/Business_and_Economy/Finance/Insurance/3.

Car Accidents

If you are in a car accident, always contact the police (dial 999) and get an accident report or the insurance company won't cover the damage. If you're not at fault, make sure you get the green copy of the report (not the pink one). Everything is in Arabic and if the other driver involved in the accident speaks Arabic and you don't, it's likely that the other driver won't tell your side of the story. Just politely wait your turn. The police officer will get to you and will hopefully understand English. Don't lose your cool. It won't do you any good.

New or Previously Owned

Most dealerships deal in both new and used cars and there are markets and car bazaars as well.

"I would definitely recommend the second-hand Car Market at Al Awir (sometimes spelled Aweer) as an excellent place to buy a car for those who don't want to buy new. Prices for second hand cars are very good here and at the market many of the main dealers have second hand showrooms," said Claire.

Some even travel to neighbouring Emirates in search of the best deals.

"I had no problem getting a licence or buying a car – except I bought it from Ras al Khaimah and had to pay twice for testing – once for it to leave RAK and again to import it into Dubai. So much for 'United' Arab Emirates," said British expat Susan Reader.

When we bought our cars we took out a loan for the first car and paid cash for the second. *Al Futtaim* took care of all of the loan details for us. If you have to deal with it yourself, there are the normal hassles of doing anything else involving banks and government departments.

Other than dealerships, *Dubizzle*, *Auto Trader UAE* (www. autotraderuae.com) and other used car sales websites are another great place to look for second hand cars for sale. On the ground, check out the supermarket bulletin boards (*Spinneys*, *Choithrams*). That's also a popular place to find houses for rent and, as I said before, maids looking for sponsorship (usually posted by the family that's leaving and wants to help find a good placement).

When weighing your options, don't forget to factor in the cost of petrol. It's usually cheaper than in other parts of the world, seeing as the UAE is an oil rich country, but the price fluctuates sometimes daily and some Emirates had shortages in the spring of 2011. With the continuing regional unrest, it's difficult to give a figure on what petrol will cost you for your car but current prices (2011) are around AED 1.7 per litre.

Road Tolls and Traffic Violations

If you are doing a budget comparison between using public transport and owning a car, don't forget to consider the cost of the road tolls known as Salik (www.salik.ae). Each time you pass through one of the four tolls along Sheikh Zayed Road, AED 4 is deducted from a pre-paid Salik account triggered by the Salik transponder you stick on your windshield. The cost to purchase the tag is AED 100, which starts you off with AED 50 in credit. You will have to fill out an application form and show your car registration. You can get an application form at most petrol stations and at select Dubai Islamic Bank and Emirates NBD branches.

Traffic violations can also add up so drive carefully. There are traffic cameras on all major roadways and the police don't even have to pull you over to present you with a ticket. Sometimes you'll get an SMS saying that you've got a ticket and to go to the Dubai Police website to pay the fine (www.dubaipolice.gov.ae). Other times you don't even know you have a fine until you go to renew your car registration. All fines must be paid before you can renew your registration (or before you can leave the country, for that matter). Fines are pretty hefty. I never got a speeding ticket but the fines are between AED 600 and AED 1,000, depending on how fast you're going. Exceeding the speed limit by more than 60 km will get you a whopping AED 2,000 fine for 'dangerous driving'. Failure to buckle up carries an AED 400 fine and talking on your mobile while driving will cost you AED 200. I found those fees out the last time I renewed our car registration. I knew it had to be my husband because I *always* put on my seatbelt and use my hands-free! But, I paid it anyways, good wife that I am.

Practicalities

If you're financing the purchase of your car with an auto loan you'll need:

- Passport (original and copy) with residence permit.

- Driving licence (original and copy).

- Bank statements for at least three months showing salary deposit.

- Salary letter from employer.

The Five-Step Recap

Step 1

Find the car of your dreams in a showroom (they're all along Sheikh Zayed Road), from the classifieds or at an auto market.

Step 2

For second hand vehicles have a mechanic check it out and have an emissions test done. EPPCO (Emirates Petroleum Products Company) has partnered with RTA to do emissions testing and safety checks.

Step 3

Secure financing (unless you're paying cash).

Step 4

Insure the car either through dealership or an insurance broker, or through your own research. We used *AXA Insurance* and they were fantastic.

Step 5

If it's a private sale, you need to complete transfer of ownership… both you and the seller will have to go in person to an RTA vehicle-licensing centre or traffic police station to make the transfer.

Tip

Once you buy your car don't forget to set up a Salik account (www.salik.ae) and attach the tag to your windshield. It's the toll that must be paid to drive on Sheikh Zayed Road. The fines for driving without it are high and build quickly as there are several tolls along the highway.

Case Study #1

"We own two cars in Dubai, both on car loans. We could have gone silly and got huge loans, but we didn't and still have two fab cars, a Golf R32 and a Land Rover LR3. The bank arranged the finance but, as with most things in Dubai, chase them constantly for updates. The roads in Dubai… well!! I consider myself a safe and confident driver. However, it did take me a couple of days to get my confidence up to go onto Sheikh Zayed Road. Nonetheless, I love driving anyway. You just have to remember that the drivers on the road in Dubai are not all trained like we are from the UK. Just make sure you use your mirrors and purchase a pair of eyes for the back of your head."

Helen from UK

Case Study #2

"We bought our car on credit card, and with the reward points flew our whole family to Europe and the Maldives. A driver's licence is easy to get, provided you don't need to re-test. Driving in Dubai has made me a better driver. As long as you stay alert and anticipate random acts of lunacy, you will be fine. A tank with a V8 is a sensible choice. Don't ever, ever flip the bird (middle finger extended), and try very hard to also avoid the emu (all five fingers held up in exasperation). If you get seen by a local doing this, you could get arrested."

The Hedonista (Sarah Walton)

Shipping a Car to UAE

There is, however, another alternative to renting or buying a car. American expat Katie Foster and her husband, Roger, actually chose to ship both their cars from Fort Lauderdale, Florida to Dubai. Very brave, indeed. Here's her story:

"The most devastating aspect of our move to Dubai was the prospect of Roger losing his newly acquired (and beloved) Corvette. Being the dutiful wife, I was determined to save the day! After careful calculations I found that there was no difference cost-wise between shipping the new Corvette and the old Ford Explorer to the UAE and selling them at a loss in the US. It seemed less daunting to ship cars we knew were in good shape than figure out how to purchase cars in a foreign country. Wise decision! After arriving we found out that we would *not* have been able to obtain car loans (as we were over 60). As with many procedures in the UAE, getting the cars through the customs office was not 'a straight line'. But I did it by myself in two days and lived to tell the tale by being patient and gracious and by acting 'blonde' and pleading 'Please help me. Don't send me home to my husband without his car'. It was a cultural ploy but it worked. Of course had I inquired around a bit, I would have found out that you can hire people to handle the process."

Katie's Steps to Making this Decision

Step 1

Make a good honest assessment of your current cars: their condition, type (are they well suited for the driving in the UAE desert climate?), what you will be able to sell them for (check the Kelly Blue Book at www.kbb.com/whats-my-car-worth) and your emotional attachment.

Step 2

Identify a reputable relocation company that ships cars to foreign countries. This may be the company that is shipping your personal belongings. Also, a quick *Google* search will give you companies that specialise in shipping vehicles.

Step 3

Determine that your cars are allowed in the country. Some restrictions apply such as the age of the car, type of tires, emissions and degree of window tinting. Note: Cars must be paid for (you must have a clear title). Check www.internationalcarshipping.net/shipping_cars_to_dubai.html.

Step 4

Work with the shipping company to calculate the shipping costs, insurance costs and duty costs, which are calculated on the value of the car. Be generous when estimating duty, as there is very likely to be additional fees of which you are unaware.

Step 5

Do the math!

Note: The shipping company, customs and duty office only take cash. Bring twice as much as you think you need.

The Wrap up

After all is said and done, if you make a decision not to buy (or ship) a car, there is public transport... and it can be fun. If you're not working and don't have kids, it's probably no big deal. If you are working, putting all the pieces together can be a chore but I remember when I lived in Toronto I lived in the suburbs and it took me two buses, a train and a subway ride to get to work and back every day (about an hour and a half each way). If you have to go to meetings in the middle of the day, then taxis are your best bet. When you put things into perspective, it tends to make sense. I'm the queen of rationalisation as well so can make the best of just about any situation. The systems are improving every day (just like the roads) and now the RTA has even added a water taxi that travels up and down the length of the creek, helping you avoid mid-day traffic in both Deira and Bur Dubai... Sweet!

Chapter 11

Registering with the Authorities – UAE National ID Card

A few years ago the UAE government decided that it would introduce a National ID card that every resident over 15 years of age (Emirati and expat) would have to have in order to receive any government related services. The Emirates Identity Authority Service Centre (EIDA, www.emiratesid.ae) was set up to manage the program and applications began. Expats are to renew annually and UAE citizens every five years.

There is still a fair bit of confusion over how and why the cards are used. The procedure has had its hiccups and the implementation of the program is still in a preliminary phase. However, government agencies and other organisations are slowly coming on board.

"I've seen signs around American Hospital that any new patients registering must show their ID cards," said American expat, blogger and travel writer, Katie Foster.

In the spring of 2011 it was announced that visa renewals at all Dubai free zones would be linked to the National ID card. It looks as though part of the reason is because clinics and hospitals are requesting it and you need a medical check up and blood tests for your residence visa. Other Emirates have already implemented the requirement for visa renewal.

Ultimately the goal is to have an accurate census count and for one card to be used as your driver's licence, health card, labour card and e-gate card (used by frequent travellers coming in and out of Dubai International Airport) but we're a far cry from that happening just yet. It brings to mind a passage I read in the book *Don't they Know it's Friday – A Cross-Cultural Guide for Business and Life in the Gulf* by Jeremy Williams:

"Attitudes were (and, in practice, remain) that God controls today and tomorrow; yesterday is over and irrelevant. Only 'now' really matters. Planning and preparation are not well-developed natural Gulf Arab characteristics. Perceptions of time, and obedience to a watch or a diary, have therefore been troublesome subjects, certainly for the older Gulf Arab, less so for the modern generation."

The deadline for everyone to have an ID card keeps getting pushed as hundreds of people missed the deadline at the end of 2010 with the system getting bogged down with requests. But, as more and more government agencies (like the RTA for car registration and driving licence) and services (telecommunications and banking) ask for it, the more urgent it will become.

Again, Emirates Airline had a special processing centre set up in the employee assistance centre to streamline the process but there were still long queues and it felt like we were being treated as if we had broken the law or something. We were photographed and fingerprinted by officious, unsmiling automatons. The things we do when we choose to live in a foreign country! But, we did choose it, so did as we were told.

If this all seems too overwhelming or you just don't have the time, there are agents you can hire to deliver documents to the typing centre and wait in line on your behalf for just about anything (I mentioned *Executive Expatriate Relocations* earlier). Once the documents are submitted and you are contacted for your appointment you will have to go in person yourself.

The Practicalities

- You'll need to complete the registration form.

- Make sure you bring your original passport (with residence visa).

- Be prepared to pay a processing fee (AED 100) plus service fee (AED 70).

Five-Step Recap

Step 1

Fill out pre-application at an approved typing centre. Bring all required documentation. They will submit the e-form to EIDA for you. You can pick up the forms at an *Empost* office but you'll have to have them filled out in Arabic at a typing office anyway.

Step 2

You will receive an SMS confirming the date and location (there are three locations in Al Barsha, Al Karama and Al Rashidiya).

Step 3

Bring your original passport to the EIDA office on the scheduled day.

Step 4

Fingerprinting will be done at your appointment.

Step 5

ID card is delivered within 7-14 days.

Tip

"Always dress ultra-conservative when visiting government offices in Dubai. I was at the RTA one day to get my will notarized and the woman at the front desk said that I had to come back and wear long pants. I wore long shorts to my knees."

Jeanette Todd, Canadian

Case Study #1

"We both went to the employee assistance centre on the same day at the same time. We were told that the cards would be delivered to our home within seven days. A week later the courier company called to say they were delivering my card and asked for directions. I told them they should have two cards, one for me and one for my wife. They only had mine. When I called to find out what had happened to hers I was told that it had been delivered to the *Empost* office in Jumeirah and I would have to pick it up."

Hal, American

Case Study #2

"When we went to get our IDs there wasn't anything extraordinary about it. We took all the paper work to the front desk at the registration centre on Hessa Street (also known as E611) in Al Barsha (it's a well-marked Dubai Municipality building) and stood in a line. We went to the typing room and stood in another line. Then we went to the finger printing room and stood in another line. Then we waited eight weeks to get them and my name was misspelled even though at each stop I told them my name was spelled wrong and each clerk said the next clerk would fix it. Oh well! There are no straight lines in Dubai!"

Katie Foster, American blogger and freelance writer

The Wrap Up

When you move to Dubai never forget that you are living in a Muslim country. There are rules to follow that you won't be used to and may seem strict at first. Two that come immediately to mind are the 'zero tolerance' for drink driving and public displays of affection (both punishable by imprisonment and/or deportation). The main purpose is to provide a safe and healthy environment for everyone, expats and locals alike. It may seem harsh or extreme but it is local law and it's advisable to follow it to the letter to avoid any unpleasant outcomes. As for the

ID card, it may feel invasive to have to 'register' with the authorities and be fingerprinted and photographed over and over again but once all the bugs are worked out, the National ID card should be the only thing you'll need to carry with you to get access to any government service in the UAE. Hopefully it will make life a little easier and not be just one more card you have to renew every year, pay a fee and add to the pile of other cards in your wallet.

Chapter 12

Setting up a Business and Renting Office Space

Opportunities to go into business for yourself in Dubai are abundant. However, the experiences I've heard about run the gamut from easy as pie (which my experience was to be quite honest) to darn near impossible.

"As an entrepreneur I find it extremely gratifying to work in Dubai. There is an entrepreneurial mindset here with lots of opportunities to meet like-minded people on the same journey," said Pam Wilson, a British expat who grew up in Zimbabwe and is managing director of *Silla,* an online community healthcare portal (www.silla.ae).

Understanding the local culture and business environment is key to prosperity in the region. There's still a lingering tribal society approach to leadership and appointments; patronage and heredity are the norm. There are myriad ways to get a business going but the most important thing to remember is that you will be doing business in an Arab country. A great reference to visit is *Culture &*

Co. (www.cultureandcompany.com) founded by Yemin-born expatriate, Wafa al Hamed. Her business helps both tourists and newcomers understand some of the nuances of Arab business behaviour. *Culture & Co.* does cultural orientation programs for businesses, provides cultural flavour for events and also does tours of the city with a focus on the UAE heritage areas.

You may also want to consider reading *Don't they Know it's Friday? A Cross Cultural Guide for Business and Life in the Gulf* by Jeremy Williams that I referenced earlier. In the forward written by Sir James Craig he says, "When you go to another man's country you have to play by his rules"… it does make it easier.

The difficult part is to figure out what those rules are. Once you do, you have to check, re-check and double check as the rules do tend to change from one day to the next and it's difficult to get a straight answer. Often times you can ask the questions and the person in the position of 'knowledge' answers with great confidence. You return the next day having followed his or her instructions only to be told that the information you were given just the day before was either inaccurate or incomplete (with no apology anywhere to be found).

"It wasn't easy to find the information about where best to set-up," says Rawan Albina, wife, mother and professional certified coach from Lebanon. "I had found the *Dubai Red Tape* book to be particularly helpful."

My decision to go into business for myself was made for me by the UAE Ministry of Labour. As of 2006, companies were banned from hiring expatriates in public relations positions (which was my expertise).

The goal is to 'Emiratise' the workforce so they were starting with specific professions. According to an article published in *Emirates 24/7* on June 29, 2011, "The rule aims to gradually replace all public relations employees in the UAE's private sector with Emiratis or citizens from the other members of the Gulf Cooperation Council (GCC)". The article, 'Firms asked not to hire expat women in PR', went on with a statement from a ministry director saying, "UAE women have proved their capability in this field and they should be given a chance… Companies which abide by these regulations will be exempt from fees on labour cards, which are set at AED 2,000 for expatriates."

I was just as happy because I was ready to launch out on my own. I chose to go through Dubai Media City (DMC) where I had a positive experience when I applied for my licence as a freelance writer. DMC is part of the Dubai Technology, E-Commerce, and Media Free Zone (TECOM) where Dubai Internet City and Dubai Knowledge Village free zones are also located. The process is similar, whether you want to be licensed as a freelancer or decide to set up an actual company (in the free zone). For either one, you'll need to submit an application that includes a business plan (for which they provide a straight forward template). TECOM seems to be one place where the guidelines are comprehensive, clear and consistent and the people I dealt with were helpful, knowledgeable and professional.

"I have worked as a consultant setting up other companies for individuals and/or companies moving to Dubai," says marketing specialist, Fiona Thomas from Scotland. "Their experiences are usually filled with frustration." However, Fiona says her own process was easy like mine. She too went through DMC.

Because of this, there is often a waiting list for DMC licences but I timed it well by applying mid-summer when many people leave and before the newcomers arrive. I researched Ras Al Khaimah (RAK) free zone as well but at the time they were re-evaluating the process. They had probably heard how much DMC was charging and were planning to increase their fees. Last I checked it was still cheaper so lots of people choose to do their licence through RAK or even Fujairah. If you don't want or need the prestige of a Dubai address and don't mind the inconvenience of driving an hour an a half every time you need to go to your 'office' to check mail, it's a good option. Since I moved to Dubai in 2007, several more free zones have been created. At last count there were more than 30 (and growing). Each one has a particular industry in which it specialises.

"The free zone people at RAK took care of all issues related to the visa so no real problems. But they needed a lot of follow-up, and securing a visa for an assistant was not trouble-free," says Irish expat Eithne Treanor, managing director of *E. Treanor Media*.

"It was easy but expensive with TECOM, Dubai Knowledge Village," said Beryl Comar, EQ development specialist, owner, *The Change Associates*, who first worked at Rashid Hospital when she moved to Dubai in 1976. "I was the first to bring hypnosis and NLP to the Middle East and now I have trained hundreds in the region to do the same."

The expense has obviously paid off for Beryl!

Benefits of free zones:

- 100% ownership (a company set up outside of a free zone requires a local partner who will own 51% of the company).

- Exemption from import duties.

- Support from free zone business centres (including employment and residence visa services).

Downside:

- You are only allowed to conduct business within that free zone or internationally (unless you have a commercial agent or distributor who will dictate the fees for their service. Fees vary dramatically, some based on a flat fee and some based on a percentage of sales or revenue, depending on what you negotiate directly with the agent or distributor).

Similarities and Differences

There are many similarities and just as many differences in the requirements between the free zones so read between the lines.

When deciding whether to set up a business and researching the whys and wherefores, there are many options. The complexities often send people running back to the security of working in-house rather than suffering through the process. However, that comes with challenges too.

"I was employed by a Pakistani-owned company. It was easy to secure my visa but I would never be under another company's sponsorship again because of the 'serfdom' attitude of some people," said Fiona. "The rules are there to help the employee but because the employee is not sure of the rules and regulations and the bosses are, the employee's ignorance is exploited. The Ministry of Labour is very proactive and is trying to make life easier by changing some of the regulations but still if you visit their offices on any working day you will see how many people have submitted official complaints."

Companies registered outside the free zones require a trade license and 51% ownership by a UAE national. You should begin your research with the Dubai Department of Economic Development (DED), at www.dubaided.gov.ae.

"Over six years, I've changed my licence on three occasions," said British expat Bijay Shah, national director, *BNI Middle East*. "From Dubai On-Shore (DED), to RAK, to TECOM. We rent office space from TECOM, which I must say is VERY expensive compared to the market. The process on each occasion has been cumbersome to say the least."

As I said, it's a real mixed bag and Vibeke Nurgberg from Denmark says it was a breeze except for the costs, which were insurmountable for her.

"In terms of setting up my own business in Dubai it was fairly easy," said Vibeke. "Dubai is still the 'land of opportunity' and with a great entrepreneurial drive. But... the sponsorship system makes it almost impossible to keep the business afloat. Either one needs a local sponsor (which is either difficult to find... or difficult to trust) or a free zone license which is a yearly cost that far exceeds the amount of money I could bring in."

As more free zones are set up, the choices increase and the ease of setting up a business improves.

"It has become so much easier to set up a business as there are companies like Virtuzone that allow you to pay monthly, have a virtual office and complete the whole process for you," said Karen Beggs from Northern Ireland. "A friend of mine has recently set up her business and it literally took her a couple of hours to do all the paperwork and formalities."

Forbes Middle East has been conducting extensive free zone studies over the past seven years and according to an article in *Emirates 24/7* on May 11, 2011, 'UAE free zones a success', TECOM leads the pack with its 'cluster' approach, bringing companies from the same industry into the same area.

Free Zones in Dubai:

- Dubai Airport Free Zone (DAFZA) - www.dafza.gov.ae

- Dubai Auto Zone - www.daz.ae

- Dubai International Financial Centre (DIFC) - www.difc.ae

- Dubai International Media Production Zone - www.impz.ae

- Dubai Logistics City - www.dwc.ae

- Dubai Maritime City - www.dubaimaritimecity.com

- Dubai Outsource Zone - www.doz.ae

- Dubai Silicon Oasis Authority (DSOA) - www.dso.ae

- International Humanitarian City - www.ihc.ae

- Jebel Ali Free Zone (JAFZA) - www.jafza.ae

- Techno Park - www.technopark.ae

- TECOM – encompasses Dubai Media City (DMC), Dubai Internet City (DIC), Dubai Knowledge Village (DKV), Dubai International Academic City, Dubai Outsource Zone, Dubai Studio City, International Media Production Zone, EnPark, DuBiotech, Dubai Healthcare City and Dubai Industrial City - www.tecom.ae

- Virtuzone – an e-office option - www.vz.ae

For an overview and updated list visit:
www.uaefreezones.com

Other resources:

- Dubai Department of Economic Development (DED)
- www.dubaided.gov.ae
  (The Department for Corporate Relations or the Promotion Centre)
- Dubai Chamber of Commerce and Industry - www.dubaichamber.com
  (Contact them to get the directory of *Standard Classification of Economic Activities*).
- Dubai Municipality - www.dubai.ae

The following options of setting up a business outside of the free zones are outlined on the DED website:

Nationals of other Arab or foreign countries may carry on economic activities through any of the following forms:

- Individual Establishment: it may be established to practice any professional activity, only by appointing a local services agent who shall be a UAE national.

- Limited Liability Company: this kind of company shall be established to carry on any commercial or industrial activity, including one or more UAE partners whose shareholding shall not be less than 51% of the paid-up capital.

- Private Shareholding Company: this kind of company shall be established to carry on any commercial or industrial activity, including one or more UAE national partners whose shareholding shall not be less than 51% of the paid-up capital.

- Civil Business Company: two or more persons may establish a civil business company to practice a profession, provided that a local services agent who must be a UAE national is appointed or included as a partner.

Any company incorporated outside the United Arab Emirates may operate any commercial, industrial or professional activity through one of the following legal forms:

- Branch of a Foreign Company

- Limited Liability Company: this kind of company shall be established to operate any commercial or industrial activity, including one or more UAE national partner whose shareholding shall not be less than 51% of the paid-up capital.

- Private / Public Shareholding Company: this kind of company shall be established to operate any commercial or industrial activity, including one or more UAE national partner whose shareholding shall not be less than 51% of the paid-up capital.

Renting Office Space

If you're setting up your business in a free zone, the office space is part of the licence agreement (which will include a rental fee for either an office, for a company, or a 'hot desk' for a freelancer).

"It was very easy to set up my business through CreativeZone. I have office space in the *Fairmont Hotel* when I need it," said Pam.

Setting up outside the free zone will require you to secure office space. You'll have to present a signed lease agreement once your application for a business licence has been approved.

"I tried to set up my own business (outside of the free zone), but have not been successful," said W Mervis, an American who has been living in Dubai for five years. "Office space is expensive and it is the one necessity if you want to be legal here. Many companies do operate illegally and don't even know it. It can be difficult to find the rules of setting up the business."

The Planning Department will have to approve your location so it's best to find out what the zoning laws are and where you can operate your type of business before you begin your search. For example, if you have an animal boarding business, you won't be able to locate your facility within the city limits. Do not sign a lease until DED has approved your location.

The Practicalities

The documentation necessary that is common among all is:

- Passport copies including residence visa (if you have one already).

- A no objection letter from your current employer (if you're transitioning from working for a company in Dubai to owning your own).

- Two passport sized photos (have more ready just in case).

- Reference letter from your bank verifying you have an account in 'good standing'.

- An updated curriculum vitae (CV).

- A notarized degree certificate.

- A comprehensive business plan (most free zones will provide a template).

- A Letter of intent.

- The proposed name of company.

- Names of shareholders and distribution of shares.

- A utility bill in your name.

The Five-Step Recap

Step 1

Decide what type of company you want to set up – free zone, freelance or LLC, sole proprietorship, or a branch of an existing company.

Step 2

Do the market research, develop your business plan, pick a company name and find a UAE partner (referred to as either a sponsor or a commercial services agent) if you're not setting up in a free zone. This individual would be responsible for taking you through all governmental procedures and for signing all application forms.

Step 3

If you decide to set up your company outside of the free zone structure, you'll need to get approval first from the appropriate ministry or government office for some business activities. Visit the DED website, click on 'Registration and Licensing' then 'Practicing Business in Dubai' for some guidance on this. You can also download the application for approval on the site.

Step 4

Submit your application with all the relevant documentation to the appropriate authority (the ministry or free zone authority you've chosen that best matches your business activity and set up option). For non-free zone companies you'll need to add, 'hunt for and secure office space' to this step.

Step 5

Take a deep breath and follow up, follow up, follow up... and pat yourself on the back for finally going it on your own. When the licence is issued, get a company stamp and register with the Dubai Chamber of Commerce, the Immigration Department and Ministry of Labour.

Tip

"The company chock (or stamp)... never leave home without it. Every company cheque requires additional signatures on the back and a stamp. If I ever answer 'no' to the question 'Have you got your company stamp with you?' there's always raised eyebrows and many others brought into the discussion, regardless of the amount of the cheque. You can get your chock in Internet City, building 3 (the *Dell* Building) at *Fix-it Express*."

Debbie Nicol, Australian, creator of *embers of the world* and managing director, *business en motion*

Case Study #1

"We founded *Heels & Deals* in 2009 just as the recession hit. We both owned our own small businesses and so many women were coming to us for advice we realised there was a tremendous need for this type of organisation. We had more than 200 women sign up for the first meeting. I guess we were doing something very positive and proactive during a time of economic, political and social uncertainty. We were getting women entrepreneurs together to share and support each other in good times and bad. Once we could afford the trade licence fee it was fairly easy to set up. We used Virtuzone (www.vz.ae) to acquire a trade licence, as they are cost-effective and efficient. We have the option of using the hot-desk facility at Virtuzone's Jumeirah Beach Residence office, however, we work mainly from home... we use technology to enable our offices to be mobile (they are wherever we are)."

Claire Fenner and Georgie Hearson, co-founders, *Heels & Deals*

Case Study #2

"I currently run my own business in professional speaking, training and business coaching based in Dubai Knowledge Village (DKV). It (the set-up) was quite easy, but not without the usual run-arounds. I contacted Knowledge Village since I was setting up a learning and development organisation. The sales staff wanted to sell me 500 square feet of space. I wanted a small office initially which they said they could not provide. So I approached DED through an agent. Again, since I was going to be in the knowledge business, I needed to comply with the Knowledge and Human Development Authority (KHDA) provisions, which seemed onerous. Luckily, DKV business centre called me again to offer the business centre proposal, which was accepted. However, since I had gotten my name approved in the interim with DED, it took me about two months to get that resolved before DKV could license me and I could start operating. I currently am well setup, 100 square feet of office space with car parking facilities. Not much else but good, efficient and suitable for my level of current operations. Keeps fixed costs down."

Shridhar Sampath, from India, owner of *Motivaluate Consulting & Training FZ LLC*

The Wrap up

From everything I've heard and from my own experience, the free zone option is the smoother, cheaper, less stress-inducing way to go. That is unless you're setting up a branch office of a large multi-national with deep pockets that's bankrolling you or you have an angel investor. The main thing is, if you have an entrepreneurial spirit, some drive and determination and a product or service that is needed, along with buckets of patience and intercultural people skills, you can successfully set up a business in Dubai. Most of the country's workforce is expats and they welcome and encourage foreign entrepreneurs to participate... you just have to play by their rules. Fair enough, right?

Chapter 13

Working from Home

When Doug and I first moved to Dubai in 2007, I had been working in the PR field for almost 20 years. The nature of the industry, revolving around media relations, events, crises and the like, requires long hours, nights and weekends and to be quite honest, I was burnt out. Like many 'trailing spouses' I took full advantage of the opportunity to take a breather. Initially, I was busy setting up the house, taking care of painters, landscapers and plumbers, cooking and cleaning while Doug was deep in the books on his course to fly the Boeing-777 for Emirates Airline. I had lots of time to myself. It was great for the first few months but then the 'career woman' inside of me started yelling to get out. The memory of the 14-hour days hadn't quite faded yet and I didn't want to re-enter the corporate world so I set about figuring out what I could do working as my own boss from the comfort of my own home.

I had read *Career in Your Suitcase* by Jo Parfitt and it inspired me to create a new career path for myself focussing on something that was portable. Our plan was to spend three to five years in Dubai and then move on to our next expat adventure, in Thailand. Full disclosure... Jo is now my publisher but I didn't know her at the time.

I evaluated my skill set by looking at all the jobs I had done in my professional life and made a list of what I was best at: media relations, event planning, crisis communications, TV/video production and writing. It was the last one that put a smile on my face. It was the least stress inducing and the most common thread amongst all the others. That was it! I would be a freelance writer. I re-worked my resumé, posted it on *MonsterGulf.com* and *Naukri.com*, printed up some business cards and started going to networking events (the first were the International Business Women's Group, IBWG, and the American Women's Association, AWA). Not long after, I landed my first two clients (Marissa Wood from *Image Factor* through AWA and David Grunfeld from *Prose Solutions* who saw my resumé on *MonsterGulf*). I was on my way!

I started to get busy and decided to go legit and applied for (and got) my freelance licence from Dubai Media City (which I told you all about in an earlier chapter). What is so exciting about my decision to re-invent myself is that I truly have a portable career now, which I can do anytime, anywhere with just a laptop, phone and an Internet connection. When I plan my next move, I'll continue to work with existing clients no matter where I am in the world and they can just pay me using PayPal or bank transfers.

Dubai is the perfect place to start exploring home business options that you can quietly test out and get going, then formalize.

"After quitting a media production job with the arrival of my son, I decided to start a project to promote traditional Yemeni arts and crafts," said British/Yemini expat Dhuha. "It was doing reasonably well until the recession hit followed now by the unrest of the region. At the moment I am focusing on completing my first novel."

We writers are pretty lucky to be able to do what we do from anywhere. All we need is the skills, a laptop, some original ideas and a client or two (or a book deal... self-publishing is always an option too).

"I got terminated, and the following morning plonked my laptop on the dining room table from where I've been working ever since," says Scottish expat and freelance writer, Jonathan Castle.

Technically, there's no such thing as a 'home office'. In order to be legitimate, all licences require office space (which could be the hot desk option at the free zones). What I chose to do, and many others I've spoken to do as well, is take the hot desk option, pop in periodically but do the bulk of my work at home. The traffic is easier to navigate, there's always parking, the Internet is pretty consistent and there's a bottomless pot of free coffee.

"When *Queen B* was a hobby I worked from home selling through craft fairs but when I wanted to release an invoice to my first retailer I needed to get my labour card and an office and work under a licensed LLC company," said Belinda Freeman, managing director, *Queen B*.

The Practicalities

Same as *Chapter 12…*

The Five-Step Recap

Step 1

Evaluate your skill set or consider what you love to do as a hobby and identify which one you're passionate about.

Step 2

Determine if it's a business that can be conducted totally online or if there's a free zone category that you fit into (maybe as a consultant through Dubai Knowledge Village or a category of specialist through DMC) or find a friend whose licence you can go under.

Step 3

Do some market research to determine whether or not there's a need for your product or skills. *Google* it, ask friends and colleagues, meet with industry people, do some networking.

Step 4

Put your business plan together. There are tons of business plan templates online but if you're researching free zones, DMC will send you a package that includes a nice template.

Step 5

If it's an online business and you are marketing to people outside of the UAE, set up a PayPal account, develop a website and go for it. If you want to do business in the UAE, refer back to *Chapter 12*.

Tip

"One thing I have learned is to focus, concentrate on one product and make it the best in the market, my greeting cards are handmade, charitable, the paper is sourced from managed forests and yes you guessed it they are priced really well."

Belinda Freeman, managing director of Queen B

Case Study #1

"When I first got married and before having the kids, I thought I would be the working kind. I had my plans set for a long career... flash forward a few years, after I had my first child, moved to Dubai then had my second son, I couldn't think of going back to a full time job and leaving the kids with someone else. No matter how I thought about it, I refused the idea of having my kids raised by someone other than myself. But I knew I had to do something to stay sane. I needed to stay active and productive but also needed the flexibility... so thought about what I most enjoyed doing and here came the idea of the business: PIES! I love being my own boss. It's a lot more work but its also very rewarding. I simply love it. Of course, as any other start up, it began small but I have to say, Dubai has a lot of potential and market niches and I'm happy that my business is growing and doing well. I love it that my product gets recognition and there is nothing more rewarding than a happy client."

Nathalie N from France, owner of *Nathalie's Pie*

Case Study #2

"There are thousands of young families who move to Dubai and many women find having young children and working full time is not so appealing and part time work is very hard to find. I, like many career driven women, had the urge to work so creating a business of my own was a perfect option allowing me to use my talents and be available for my children. My husband came up with *Queen B* as my name is Belinda. It stuck and I started the trademark process immediately. I faced some tough opposition from Buckingham Palace and Queen (The band) but after two years we managed to successfully secure the (trade) mark, which lasts for 10 years.

Finding a gap in the market came second and I felt greeting cards in the UAE were very expensive so I started to make them myself. This was pre-children while working full time as a fashion designer. A friend told me I should try selling them at a monthly craft market. I also attended as many house parties, school fairs, fetes and networking events as possible to perfect my sales techniques and get the brand out. When my second child arrived I felt it was time to stop the full time job as my maternal demands were now so much greater and this would give me the opportunity to grow *Queen B*.

With a popular collection of over 70 designs and thousands of cards sold I felt confident enough to approach a local company to work under their sponsorship so that I could issue invoices legally to stores. Within a year, I secured 22 stores including five *Virgin Megastores*. My plan for the future is to build on my collection, grow the brand so that it is available in hundreds of stores globally and work with mothers who want to sell cards at their own coffee morning events."

Belinda Freeman, managing director, *Queen B*

The Wrap up

There's a huge movement afoot of people telecommuting and setting up home businesses so there are plenty of examples to follow. You certainly have to be careful doing your research as there are so many scams that claim you can make thousands of dollars a month for doing practically nothing, sitting on your butt at home. Just review those with a critical eye. I found a great resource at www.entrepreneur.com and one of the articles lists the 10 ways to grow your home-based business. It's chock full of great ideas and helpful references. There are some great examples already in Dubai and I suggest going to a *Heels & Deals* meeting for some inspiration. Every single member either has her own business, is contemplating starting one or is a consultant and is willing to share her experiences with you.

Chapter 14

Connecting the Family - Your Health and Wellbeing

If lady luck is smiling down on you, your employer may include healthcare benefits in your employment package. Often times, the package will include a list of doctors, dentists, hospitals, clinics and specialists that are included in the coverage. We were extremely lucky that Emirates Airline actually has a clinic just for employees and their families staffed with primary care doctors and specialists, including dentists. I had only great experiences with the clinic. My only complaint would be that every time I went, I saw a different doctor. For someone with on going issues or with a history of a serious problem like a heart condition, this might be a little unsettling.

"My doctor in the USA found me a specialist in Dubai and I have used this specialist to find other doctors as needed. I mainly use the American Hospital because of the high quality of care and compassion received from all the staff and the ease of processing everything from appointments to prescriptions to billing. I met my dentist at an AWA meeting and she is excellent," said American expat, Katie Foster, freelance writer and blogger.

You never know where you're going to meet the right person at the right time and Dubai is full of these chance meetings. But, you certainly can't leave your and your family's health to chance.

"The biggest challenge when moving to Dubai was finding the right doctor for my three-month-old," said Shridhar Sampath from India. "I lived in Jebel Ali and at that time (2001) there weren't many clinics in my area. For a vaccination when we visited one of the clinics we had a rookie doctor who did a very poor job. My daughter still has the scars from that vaccination."

Dubai is a thriving city and with that comes the need to focus on the health and wellbeing of citizens and residents (a huge number of whom are expats who put healthcare high up the checklist when considering a move to a new country). Healthcare systems around the world are in a state of flux so when comparing quality of care, I'm going to go out on a limb and say, in general, it's pretty good in Dubai. All healthcare facilities in Dubai must have international accreditation. And, there are processes in place to help those who experience any medical malpractice. Of course, nothing is perfect.

"If you need basic healthcare such as childbirth it is no problem," says Marissa Wood, British expat, personal brand expert and entrepreneur who has been living in Dubai since 1977 "If you have any rare disorder that needs special attention, travel abroad. All the nationals do and that says a lot."

I'm happy to say, I didn't have anything serious happen to me (touch wood) but visited friends in a couple of hospitals (MedCare hospital and WellCare) so have seen the level of care from an 'outside looking in' perspective.

"I would wholeheartedly endorse MedCare Hospital as I have gone there for emergency care more than once and was extremely well taken care of," said Debbie Nicol. I actually visited Debbie while she was there (both times) and found it a pleasant environment (well… as pleasant as a place can be that's full of sick and injured people).

"I find personal referrals one of the best sources for finding healthcare professionals because people are generally careful about who they recommend," offers Claire Fenner.

The best advice in any situation is to do the research and referrals are always a good idea. But remember that everyone's experience is going to be different and choosing a doctor is a personal decision. A great place to start your search is using an amazing resource called *Silla* (www.silla.ae), an online healthcare portal that was created by expat entrepreneur, Pam Wilson from Zimbabwe, to connect people to healthcare services in the region. Remember Pam? She's offered some great advice in previous chapters.

"I have lived in Dubai for nine years and throughout this time I have had very positive experiences with regard to healthcare practitioners," said Pam. "I started to notice, however, that my friends and their friends sometimes had less than satisfactory experiences."

Pam created *Silla* to be a social recommendation engine that helps you find the best healthcare practitioners in the UAE.

"Clearly there were great practitioners in Dubai but perhaps others were not providing acceptable levels of service according to some of their patients," said Pam. "In this scenario, we have to take into account that we all have personal preferences with regard to how we are treated. Some of us have no time to waste and prefer a practitioner who gets straight to the point and our visit is quick and unemotional. Others prefer our healthcare providers to remember us, ask us the status of our previous ailment and whether our kids are enjoying the summer."

When developing *Silla*, Pam took all of this into account and built a portal where the community can recommend their own practitioner, according to their experiences and preferences, allowing others who read their recommendation to choose which healthcare provider suits them.

If your company does not provide healthcare coverage you can apply to the Ministry of Health (www.moh.gov.ae) for a health card to give you access to public, government run, healthcare services. There will be fees charged for the services but it will usually be lower than going to a private hospital and you can, of course, purchase insurance. There's a great information source online of the public healthcare facilities in Dubai at the Dubai Health Authority (www.dohms.gov.ae).

The public hospitals are not allowed to deny emergency medical care to anyone (whether or not you have a health card). If you do have an emergency, dial 999. For regular check ups and non-emergency care you'll either pay as you go, be covered under a company plan or purchase your own medical insurance. There are many providers to choose from so, again, research and referrals are key. As I said earlier, we used *AXA Insurance* for our car and they were fantastic (and reasonably priced). If they handle their medical insurance clients in the same way, I can highly recommend them but there are several companies to choose from.

"I use *Bupa International*," said Debbie. "They're very good and I've never had a medical claim knocked back. I've used *ADNIC (Abu Dhabi National Insurance Company)* as well and they were fine, but I prefer *Bupa*."

Doctor-Dubai has a lengthy list of insurance companies and contact information at www.doctor-dubai.com/InsuranceCompaniesDubai.asp?page=1. When you hear people say you can get anything you want in Dubai, for a price, they mean it. And, you never know where you're going to find it. It may even be right on your front doorstep.

"There's an internal medicine and dentistry practice in our building that turned out to be very good," said American expat, Shirley W Ralston (MA/Christian Education) who lives in Dubai Marina.

The Practicalities

If you apply for a public health card you'll need:

- Passport copy with copy of the residence visa page.

- Letter from sponsor (company or spouse).

- Two passport sized photos (remember those?).

- Application (which must be picked up and filled out in person at one of the public hospitals – Dubai Hospital, Rashid Hospital or Al Wasl Hospital).

- Your Tenancy agreement.

Note: Your card will have on it the location of the public hospital and/or clinic nearest to you.

To apply for healthcare insurance:

- Once you choose the company you want, they will determine your eligibility (UAE resident, no previous illnesses, no current insurance).

- Passport copy with copy of the residence visa page.

- Application (most companies have online applications you can download).

- Medical report (some require a full physical exam including blood tests and x-rays).

The Five-Step Recap

Step 1

Check with your company whether or not your employment package includes medical coverage. If not, try to negotiate an insurance allowance.

Step 2

Ask neighbours, co-workers, new friends, your concierge or any local web discussion forums, the names of their primary care physician, dentist, paediatrician (or any other specialist you may need) and if they would recommend them.

Step 3

Gather names of insurance companies, review requirements, costs and coverage. Compare and contrast and choose your provider. Find out if the doctors recommended are on the coverage plan.

Step 4

Visit the offices of the recommended health care providers, interview staff and doctor and confirm that they do indeed take your insurance. Or, if you really like them, you may choose to pay as you go and use the insurance for any hospital care or medications.

Step 5

Stay healthy!

Tip

Dubai actually has a service offered by Jebel Ali Hospital, where you can call for a doctor to make a house call for AED 500 per visit (you must pay cash but the doctor will sign a claim form if you have medical insurance). It's available to anyone... residents or visitors. 800-DOCTOR (362867) www.800doctor.com.

Case Study #1

"Interestingly, some things are remarkably easier here in Dubai than at home when it comes to being ill – namely – getting your hands on some antibiotics. For instance, when I had pink eye in Houston, I had to go to an optometrist for two visits (pay around $250) and pay for my prescription of eye drops ($25). Then my insurance declined my claim for the optometrist because I didn't first get a referral from a general practitioner. Are three doctor visits really necessary to diagnose and treat pink eye? Apparently not in Dubai. Here, I just walked into a pharmacy, spent $3 on the same antibiotic eye drops I bought in Houston, and went on my merry way."

American expat, Lynda Skok Martinez from her blog, *Longhorns and Camels*

Case Study #2

"One great thing about Dubai is that you can make an appointment for an MRI or to see a specialist and get in the next day. You'll pay, but it's often more affordable than you'd expect. Also, pharmacies are well stocked and you can get much more over-the-counter in terms of antibiotics than you can back home. My husband's company provides a health centre with docs, nurses and dentists for its employees. These folks are relatively underpaid, so the clinics are chronically understaffed. The company definitely presents its healthcare package as a benefit but overall I'm disappointed with the reality. Also, if you're married and on birth control, get ready to have to obtain your husband's permission for your next prescription."

Amy from Canada

The Wrap up

No matter where your next expat adventure takes you the feedback you're going to get on the healthcare system of your new country will be varied (like the input from all the *@Home in Dubai* survey respondents). I grew up in Canada with socialised medicine that's supposed to be the envy of the world but you'll get just as many varied stories of people who have had great experiences with it and those who have died waiting for specialised treatment. I also lived in the US for 14 years where there's definitely a two-tiered system. If you can pay for it, you can get it. That's pretty much how it is in Dubai too.

Chapter 15

Connecting the Kids

Finding a School

Seeing as the only kid I have is the four-legged, furry kind, I'll have to defer to the experts (parents and professionals) for the most part on this one. However, I will share an opinion here and there (I just can't help myself). I did study early childhood education and worked in the field before I became a PR professional, so that's how I'll claim to be qualified to weigh in on the subject.

From my perspective and from what my friends with kids tell me, there is a lot for kids to do in Dubai (check out www.dubaikidz.biz, a great online resource for parents, and click on 'Things to do'). But, I'm going to go out on a limb and guess that the first priority in connecting your kids when you move to Dubai is to find a school. The experiences vary greatly so brace yourself to do the legwork since you do know your kids best.

Public schools here are only for locals (and some GCC

citizens) so you have no choice than to find the right private school. They all have waiting lists so start the research before you move here for good and try to visit schools in advance. Maybe you can fit it in when you come for your interview. If you've already made the move, don't sweat it. Just listen, learn and ask lots of questions of those who have done it before.

"Although Aryan was born in Dubai, we are still facing challenges with finding a place in a suitable school for him. He has been on a waiting list in two schools for over two years," said Bijay Shah, national director of *BNI Middle East*.

Bijay's experience is not unusual but, don't despair, there are so many schools in Dubai, and more open every year but be prepared to compromise just a bit. Each year, the Dubai Schools Inspection Bureau (DSIB) does an extensive survey of both public and private schools. It rates them Outstanding, Good, Acceptable or Unsatisfactory; publishes a report; and makes it available to the public. It's posted on the Knowledge and Human Development Authority website (www.khda.gov.ae). The 2011 report compares results from surveys conducted over the past three years. I may not have kids but as a PR and marketing professional I know a thorough report when I see one so, in my non-maternal opinion, this would be a good place to start understanding what's on offer here.

When perusing the report, it's hard not to notice that all of the 'Outstanding' schools are using the British curriculum.

The private schools listed in this category in the 2010-2011 report included: *Dubai College* (www.dubaicollege. org), *Jumeirah College* (www.gemsjc.com), *Jumeirah English Speaking School* (www.jess.sch.ae), *GEMS Jumeirah Primary School* (www.jumeirahprimaryschool. com), *GEMS Wellington International School* (www. wellingtoninternationalschool.com) and *Kings Dubai School* (www.kingsdubai.com). Of course, I'm sure this won't be the only deciding factor. When choosing your child's school, there's so much to be taken into consideration.

"Moving a family overseas is exciting but can be fraught with challenges," says educational consultant Becky Grappo who has lived and worked in Dubai and several other countries, is an expat entrepreneur and mother of three Third Culture Kids herself. "Probably the most anxiety provoking is finding the right school for the kids. Each of your children has different needs. One may be in the last years of high school, one may have learning differences, and one may be extremely gifted and hungry for a bigger challenge. And on top of all of this, your children are becoming Third Culture Kids, which adds an additional layer of complexity to the equation," Becky adds. "The key is to know before you go."

Knowing and understanding are two very different things and long-time Dubai resident Marissa Woods reminds newcomers that it's not going to be the same as you may be used to at home.

"My son is about to start nursery and with my mother's 20 or so years' background in teaching in the UAE, I had an insider's viewpoint on the best learning environments," said Marissa. "The only issue is that not all schools (the majority!) have learning at the heart of their calling, as most are commercial entities, which is a real learning for new expats from the western 'free society, children's needs come first' environment."

Country-Connected Curricula

As you begin your research you'll find that the beauty of Dubai here again is the fact that the majority of the population is expats, so schools cater to many different languages, cultures and curricula. There are schools for just about any nationality including American, British, Indian, Lebanese and French.

"Being French, the choice was limited to French schools as I wanted my children to have French as a first language, so went straight to the *French Lycée Pompidou* (www. lfigp.org)," said Nathalie N from France.

The curricula on offer are equally diverse, ranging from American and British to International Baccalaureate.

"Since my daughter was going to be a senior in high school and she came from an American school with an AP (advanced placement) curriculum, we looked for an

American school with an AP curriculum. That is how we chose *American School of Dubai* (www.asdubai.org)," said Shirley W Ralston.

Because of long waiting lists, often times the decision is made for you (which is where the compromise I mentioned before comes in).

"I asked the Danish Consulate for advice, called the schools in the area I wanted to live and only one had room for us," said Rike Ebel Nielsen from Denmark.

Both of *Heels & Deals* co-founder, Claire Fenner's, boys were born in Dubai and started schooling at nursery level. Her eldest one is in primary school. "I put our first sons' name down for *JESS* (*Jumeirah English Speaking School*) Arabian Ranches when he was six months old and he didn't even get on the wait list," said Claire. "Luckily we had also put him down for *Dubai British School* (www. dubaibritishschool.ae) and he is very happy there."

For blogger, The Hedonista (Sarah Walton), her four year-old went to *GEMS Wellington Primary School* (www. gemswps.com) for kindergarten. "It was one of the only schools we could get him into at that point. We were lucky. It has been a good choice and our second son starts there in September (2011). Many of his friends moved to other schools, particularly *Kings*, *Repton* (www.reptondubai. org) and *JPS* (*GEMS Jumeirah Primary School*)."

According to an article in the *Gulf News* (www.gulfnews.com) titled, 'Increasingly Hard to get into Dubai's Good Schools', on April 22, 2011, "long waiting lists at schools do not always reflect the demand since many parents apply to a number of schools at the same time". So, even if there's a waiting list, if it's the school you want, go through the motions but always have more than one back up.

The List of Choices Grows

"Both my children completed their schooling here and then went on to university. They both attended international schools (*Dubai College* and *Dubai American Academy*, www.gemsaa-dubai.com) which I had heard were good schools," said Padmini Sankar, long-time Indian expat.

If your children are nursery school age the competition for spots is just as stiff. A lady who came to look at a desk I was selling (who was pregnant and expecting her third child soon) said her eldest son went to *Children's Oasis Nursery* (www.childrensoasisnursery.com). When she first applied there was a long waiting list but the head mistress said to come in for an interview anyway. On the day of the interview the list miraculously disappeared and they had a spot. The mom speculated that it was because her son 'fit the mould'. Profiling in nursery school admissions? Say it isn't so!

He apparently enjoyed his year there and now he's registered to attend *Raffles* in the fall, which wasn't her first choice but she lamented that she had left it too late. The same mom suggested toddler moms check out *Horizon Primary* (www.horizonschooldubai.com), *Star International* (http://starschoolmirdif.com) and *Jebel Ali Primary* (www.jebelalischool.org) for pre-school and primary programs.

The Practicalities

- You'll need passport copies for each child along with copies of their residency visas.

- Some schools require the child write an entrance exam and most will have an interview/assessment process.

- Make sure you have copies of all your child's school records.

- Make sure you discuss any learning support needs your child might have. Some schools may not have appropriate special needs programs. If they do, it can be extremely costly and is not likely covered by your company's schooling allowance.

The Five-Step Recap

Step 1

During salary and benefit package discussions, make sure you negotiate a schooling allowance for all children who are in pre-kindergarten to 12th grade.

Step 2

Make a list of priorities (curriculum, language, proximity, special needs programs, extra-curricular activities, class size, teacher training and accreditation, for example). Break your list down into 'must have' and 'not imperative to the health and wellbeing of my child and/or my sanity'.

Step 3

Review the schools in the Knowledge and Human Authority report; gather recommendations from co-workers and company liaison (or employee assistance centre/HR department), neighbours and friends.

Step 4

Review websites of schools that meet your requirements, make contact and schedule a meeting and tour.

Step 5

Gather all documentation required to make application.

Tip

School fees can be pretty hefty so try to negotiate that into your benefits package as well (if not the full amount, at least a subsidy).

Case Study #1

"My daughter goes to secondary school in an International Baccalaureate school and my son attends nursery. Finding schools was relatively easy. We came to Dubai four months prior to our move and saw this school and another one. My daughter took the assessment test and was admitted. For my son it was also relatively easy. We more or less knew which area we would be looking for houses in so we tried for schools and nurseries in the area so that I wouldn't have to spend all morning dropping off and all afternoon picking up. It proved to be a wise choice as you can easily drive A LOT in Dubai. My son handled the move extremely well. My daughter was a bit more hesitant but handled the move fine. However, once the first two months in school was over the magic of moving to another country vanished into thin air and the hard facts of life hit her: the loss of the friends back home and the familiar surroundings, losing the sense of freedom (I have to drive her everywhere) and the different school system. My daughter is still struggling to settle in. One piece of good advice to all parents: do think twice about moving abroad with a teen if you haven't done it before. And reconsider if Dubai really is the place to go. Had I known what I know now about the heartache my daughter suffers I'm not sure we would have moved at all."

Vibeke Nurgberg, Danish National

Case Study #2

"Before leaving Singapore, I trawled the Internet for schools that could offer the International Baccalaureate (IB) diploma curriculum and subject match that my son needed to continue his post-16 studies as well as one that could accommodate both (secondary school-aged) children. We wanted them to go to the same school and share the same experiences and at least know someone at school on the first day. I looked at the IB website (www. ibo.org) which lists schools offering the IB and then set about reviewing each school's website and trawling forums (such as www.expatwoman.com) for comments relating to them. Family life means just that for us. We wouldn't have contemplated a life where parents might live apart or children board, so we all came together, despite it not being a great time in a young adult life to move. But hey, the teenagers have been great, throwing themselves into expat life and maxing out on *Facebook* and SMS to keep in touch with friends back in the gateway to Asia! After all, as someone once said to me, it's not the making friends that's difficult, it's the saying 'goodbye'."

Mary James, wife, mother, and itinerant market sleuth from England

The Wrap up

It's only after the critical steps have been accomplished, like getting the visas and work permits, finding a home, getting the kids into school, lining up medical coverage and such that you even start thinking about having some fun. I'd suggest that you at least have a quick look at the 'Things to do' list at *Dubai Kidz* (or www.timeoutdubai. com/kids) and intersperse some fun early on in the process. It will make connecting to your city so much easier for both you and the kids and help everyone blow off some steam due to the stresses you're feeling. My favourites are Ski Dubai (www.skidxb.com) and Wild Wadi (www. jumeirah.com/hotels-and-resorts/Wild-Wadi). Let's just say, I'm a big kid at heart.

Chapter 16

The Pet Connection

If one of your family members is a cat or a dog, be prepared to put together just as much documentation as you would for any other dependent moving to Dubai with you. The rules will vary depending on what country you are coming from so make sure you check the United Arab Emirates Ministry of Environment and Water, Animal Health Department (www.moew.gov.ae). Check to see if the country you're moving from has any restrictions and whether or not you have a breed that's been banned from the UAE (all pit bulls, some mastiffs, wolfs and some dog hybrids are not allowed into the country). All animals must come in as cargo, not as checked or excess baggage and never in the cabin with you (unless it's a seeing eye dog which can travel with you in the cabin at no extra charge on direct flights to or from the US or Canada).

We have your regular garden-variety domestic cat named Zorro. It truly cost an arm and a leg to get him to Dubai. We love our pets, don't we? We complicated matters by spending some time in Canada before we headed overseas so we needed documentation from the appropriate US government agency as well as the Canadian contingent (all for a fee, of course). Zorro is better documented than any immigrant in history. We call him robo-cat sometimes as he has the obligatory microchip nestled under the skin between his shoulder blades.

It is possible to complete the pet import process yourself but at one point or another you need someone on the ground in Dubai to go in and pay for the permit in person and collect the animal at Cargo Village (which can be difficult to navigate especially if you're arriving at night, but it is an option). We decided it was far too complicated and handed the process over to *Dubai Kennel and Cattery* (www.dkc.ae), who did a great job and delivered him to our door upon arrival (there's no quarantine on domestic pets unless the animal is under four months of age).

The Practicalities

- All vaccinations (dogs need canine distemper, canine parvo virus, infectious canine hepatitis and leptospirosis and cats need FPV, feline rhinotrachitics and feline calicivirus) and rabies shots must be up to date (no older than one year or more recent than 30 days) and, from some countries, the animal will be required to travel with the original rabies vaccination certificate.

- Your passport copy and residence permit.

- An international health certificate done by a government veterinarian in your home country (or wherever you're departing from) not more than 48 hours before departure.

- The animal will need to be micro-chipped.

- The animal will have to be sent by cargo using an approved shipping company (from Canada we used SeaAir International).

- The UAE Import Permit (Pet Animals) is only valid for one month.

The Five-Step Recap

Step 1

Apply for the import permit either yourself or through a pet importer such as DKC.

Step 2

Have your animal get all the appropriate shots and get original rabies certificate.

Step 3

Make arrangements with cargo shipping company.

Step 4

Two days before departure, bring the animal to government vet for examination and health certificate.

Step 5

Travel to Dubai and pick up your pet at Cargo Village. Register your pet with the Dubai municipality. You can go yourself or a local vet can do it for you.

> **Tip**
> My vet told me not to worry because a cat sleeps 18 hours a day and once all the activity died down and the kennel was loaded and the doors closed, he'd go to sleep. She also said not to drug him because if there were any turbulence, he'd need his wits about him to brace himself.

Case Study #1

"For a fee, there are kennels in Dubai that will meet your dogs at the airport and deliver them to your home. However, if you want to collect your dogs yourself, it is fairly straightforward. Go to the cargo village. I cannot remember where exactly but it was towards the end on the right hand side. Your dogs will be taken to a special holding area that is air-conditioned. Once you have confirmed that the flight has landed, and your dogs are off the airplane, you need to alert the duty vet that you require his services. His mobile number will be on his desk. He will go and look at the dogs, give them a quick examination and check the paperwork. He will then inform you that you can collect your dogs. At this point you need to hire a truck and driver (there are always plenty around the cargo village, but you need to make sure they are happy to transport animals) and then find a porter with a large enough trolley to transport the dog(s) in their boxes to the truck. This is probably less difficult than it sounds. I had a two-year-old in tow and didn't find it too challenging. Everyone was very helpful and interested. Remember to get the truck driver's mobile number and licence plate number, assuming you are not traveling in the truck as well. As you exit the cargo village the paperwork will be checked one more time and then you are free to go. Our dogs seemed unaffected by their journey and arrival in Dubai. However a friend's dog, of the same breed and temperament, was quite traumatized and took a week to get back to normal."

Leigh, Dubai Women's College, Expat Info

Case Study #2

"We were living in Cairo in early 2011 when the revolution broke out. My husband's company evacuated us on an American Express charter flight and we had no idea where we were going until we were on the plane. We each grabbed one small carry on and, Minnie, our Yorkshire terrier. Leaving her wasn't an option. We got on the plane and were told that we were going to London. I planned to just to take the dog with us through customs and be on our way. I had her in a small carrier and she didn't make a peep. It wasn't until two days later that immigration came knocking on the door at the hotel and demanded that I hand over the dog that I had 'smuggled' into the UK! At the same time, we were waiting for my husband's company to make the final arrangements for a transfer to Dubai. We had tickets to fly from London to Dubai in less than a week but Minnie had to be quarantined for at least 25 days before we could bring her to the UAE. Egypt has a rabies problem and since she originated there, the rabies shots she had less than seven months before didn't count. The tests they had to run took 25 days to show results and determine that she was clear. If we had been staying in London she would have been quarantined for six months (although that law is supposed to be lifted in January 2012). Even once that was done, we still couldn't bring her to Dubai because we were staying at a hotel and in the UAE it's illegal to have a dog in a hotel (even if the hotel is pet friendly in other parts of the world). After jumping through several hoops we finally had her with us by mid-April after providing all the documentation needed, which seemed like a moving target."

Patty Axelsen, American

The Wrap Up

The stories I hear about people's decisions to move with or without animals (both coming in and leaving Dubai) range from 'there's no way I'd leave Cuddles behind' to families who choose to put elderly animals to sleep or leave them with relatives in their home country rather than putting them through the trauma of a move overseas. It's not an easy decision but you know your pet best. Zorro handled the 24-hour journey in his kennel like a champ but I have heard others claim that their pet was never the same again. It's just another item to add to the checklist and another connection that needs to be made.

Chapter 17

Connecting – Virtually

Mobile Phones and SIM cards

A lot of people I know by-pass the hassle of getting a landline at home and simply operate with a mobile phone. It's pretty easy to get one, the cost is reasonable (if you don't want a data package or call internationally on a regular basis) and you don't need a residence visa for the pre-paid option. Stop by a Marhaba counter when you land in Dubai and ask where you can get a temporary, three-month mobile number to carry you through until you're set up. Most electronics retailers will also sell SIM cards with a local number.

Same as your landline, you have two options: *Etisalat* (www.etisalat.ae) and *du* (www.du.ae). The majority of my survey respondents (65%) use *Etisalat*. That's most likely because it has been around longer and there are communities where you don't have a choice.

Both have pre and post-paid options. Personally, I used *Etisalat's* WASL pre-paid program, which I prefer to a monthly bill. No muss, no fuss and it includes voicemail and SMS. No surprises at the end of the month (I know... I sound like a marketing message but I can't help it, it's in my blood). You can roam internationally to some countries but check the list before you travel.

Some months I used more than others but typically, I spent about AED 150 a month. I was able to check the amount remaining any time I wanted by dialling 121 and it was easy as pie to top it up. The payment was connected to our bank account so I could just go in to my account and in about three clicks I added what I needed. You can also get WASL minutes from just about any gas station, department store or supermarket and at any *Etisalat* business centre. As for the phone itself, I picked it up cheap at *Carrefour* (www.carrefouruae.com) in the Mall of the Emirates and it came with the SIM card.

I came across many others who feel the same way as I do.

"I use *Etisalat*. I'm happy with the cell phone service," said Mary-Alison Lyman from Canada. "But the lines in the stores are always ridiculous so I use pay as you go to avoid having to visit stores."

With only two options, there's not a whole lot of competition and from one month to the next both *Etisalat* and *du* add new plan offerings to attract new customers. However, once you've chosen one, there's often little to entice you to change because the differences aren't that big.

"I got my SIM card with *Etisalat* when I first arrived and while I think *du* does better value packages now, I can't be bothered going through the hassle of changing accounts and getting a new phone number," said Australian, Kara Boden.

Freelance writer Jonathan Castle echoed Kara's sentiments. "I use *Etisalat* purely for historical reasons. There was no alternative when I got my number, and now there are too many people who use it to make changing it worthwhile," said Jonathan who hails from Scotland.

Then there's the decision between pre and post-paid. My husband got a monthly bill and had a data package too and he was constantly trying to figure out the bill, convinced they were seriously overbilling him. There's no way to prove or disprove it so it's your word against theirs. I stick to my belief that simpler is better here, so I'm keeping with the pre-paid option no matter where we live. But that doesn't work for everyone.

"I use *Etisalat* for my phone," says Helen from the UK. "They seem to be good value for using the Blackberry. I pay approximately AED 250 a month for all calls, texts and emails."

Helen's fellow Brit, Karen Beggs has had similar experience with the competitor. "I use *du* for my mobile and generally find it very good. My bills are approximately AED 200 per month and that is with the occasional call to the UK!"

As with any product or service, the more bells and whistles you want, the more you're going to pay.

"I have *Etisalat* for my mobile and it is fair value for the money," said Alba Micheli Geddes from Italy. "The drawback is that I had to leave a deposit of AED 1,000 to have international roaming."

One of my biggest bugaboos with the mobile phone service in Dubai is, since there's so little competition, both companies are merciless with their spamming. And, I'm not alone in my angst.

"They constantly bombard me with Spam text messages," said British expat Susan Reader. "It's a nightmare and there is no way to stop them. Apparently *Etisalat* sold all their numbers to a third party that is willing to pay for them."

The set-up challenges will be slightly less than when you set up the landline since they already have all your particulars but it's the billing that can then be a little problematic.

"It was a struggle at first to get things set up correctly and I still cannot pay my bill online but overall, it's acceptable," says American expat, Shirley W Ralston who uses *du*.

Connecting with Customer Service

The level of customer service fluctuates from one day to the next and everyone seems to have a wide range of experiences.

"I use *du*. When I first arrived everyone said *du* was rubbish and not to go with them. So I used *Etisalat* and still have the number but rarely use it. *du* is better at providing an all round reasonable experience and at least try to be helpful," says Fiona Thomas a marketing specialist from Scotland.

How 'helpful' they are often depends on the severity of the problem you're experiencing and whether or not the person on the other end of the line has dealt with your particular issue before. If they haven't, be ready for the all-too-familiar final answer, "I'm sorry, you'll have to come into the main service centre to resolve that problem."

"I use *Etisalat*. It's okay when things are going right but when things go wrong you have to deal with their dire customer (dis)service crew which is more painful than sticking hot needles in your eyes! I think the customer service policy is to annoy you so much you don't bother them again," says Susan Castle, from Scotland.

Hopefully you're experience will fall more under Fiona's category of customer service rather than Susan's.

The Practicalities

For pre-paid you'll need:

- A copy of your passport (and residence visa or visit visa stamp).

- Subscription fee.

For post-paid you'll need:

- Passport copy with valid residence visa.

- UAE work permit.

- Salary letter indicating that monthly income is more than AED 5,000.

Note: For either plan you must be over 21.

The Five-Step Recap

Step 1

Upon arrival at the airport (or as soon as you can) purchase a temporary SIM card with a local phone number. You'll be glad you did. Ask at the *Marhaba* Counters at the Dubai Airport or the *UAE Exchange* outlets.

Step 2

Research whether or not your existing phone can be used in the UAE (especially if you have an iPhone or Blackberry that might be locked by your previous provider). If it can't be used, it's time to go shopping.

Step 3

Review plans on offer from both *Etisalat* and *du* and compare prices for both pre-paid and post paid services. Don't forget to check the roaming and data packages and ask how the billing works. You don't want any surprises.

Step 4

When you go to buy your phone, some retailers will have plans on offer right there in the store. You want to know the comparable plans so you can make the right decision.

Step 5

If you already have a phone you can use, visit any *Etisalat* or *du* outlet, post office or mobile phone store (you can find both in most malls… and there are loads of those to choose from) to purchase your SIM card and initiate your plan.

Tip

No matter what you may face, "Keep your feet on the ground and always remember to be respectful of the place, the people and the culture," advises Claire Fenner, co-founder, *Heels & Deals*. This goes along nicely with a Dutch Proverb I came across recently: "A handful of patience is worth more than a bushel of brains."

Case Study #1

"I use *du* for my mobile phone but it took a lot to understand the most economical way to go since it was so different from plans in the US. I did not get an international calling plan as we use *magicJack* to call home. I came with my iPhone which I discovered was 'locked' and when I had it unlocked I negated my warranty. People should be warned about bringing their USA Smart Phone here as there are problems."

Katie Foster, American blogger and freelance writer

Case Study #2

"Georgie and I are on the *du* Her Super Business Plan which is a special plan for women entrepreneurs and women professionals. The plan is only AED 200 a month and I receive 400 minutes of national calls, 200 minutes international calls, a mobile data package and free calls to other women on the same plan."

Claire Fenner, co-founder, *Heels & Deals*

The Wrap up

Although I am a self-admitted techno-geek and love new technology and love to learn new computer programs (that relate specifically to what I do for a living that might make my life easier), until recently I had a tiny *Samsung* flip phone that I bought when we first arrived in Dubai. For almost four years, it did everything I needed it to do and I saved bundles of money on data downloads. Point being, you can have mobile communications quite cheap in Dubai if you stick to the basics. If you need to have a 24/7 access to your emails; ability to immediately communicate with everyone you've ever met in your life; a GPS that goes everywhere you go; and other nifty games and toys at your fingertips on a whim, then you can have that too for a price.

Chapter 18

Wi-Fi Hotspots

My one and only foray into finding a Wi-Fi hotspot in Dubai was during my first week here. I sat surrounded by boxes in the first villa we were assigned by the company. It was, according to my husband, unacceptable due to the fact that it was on the edge of the compound and the bedroom window faced a main thoroughfare. He's a light sleeper and knew that it would be disastrous for him with the crazy schedule he would be working where he would have to sleep at odd hours of the day.

So, I sat there, fingers itching to start unpacking but unable to do so while we begged and pleaded to be moved. So, what to do? The Internet wasn't hooked up yet and we had no TV as we expected the call any day to switch villas so everything was on hold. I couldn't surf the Net, check my emails, *Facebook* my friends and family. Eeek!

"Find a Wi-Fi hotspot," was Doug's helpful suggestion. "We're right next to Media City so there's bound to be a bunch. Just walk over," he called over his shoulder as he left in our rental car to go to class.

I sat there in a daze. I was still jetlagged. I didn't want to walk to Media City but the longer I sat there stewing over not being able to surround myself with my familiar stuff, the more irritated I became. So, I headed out. It was December so it wasn't too hot but my computer bag was heavy and I was in a mood. I walked around the corner only to come face to face with what was, at the time, a dusty construction zone spreading as far as the eye could see.

"Excuse me," I stopped a random person walking by. "Can you tell me where I might be able to access a wireless signal?" I held up my laptop to illustrate my need.

"That way," he pointed towards a grouping of buildings. "At the *Radisson Hotel*."

"Thanks!" I was relieved as I set out thinking I would see a sign any minute pointing me to the oasis that would be the *Radisson*. I walked for several minutes and didn't see any buildings that remotely resembled a hotel or even a building that was finished and open. I gave up and returned to the villa and broke open the box that was labelled 'books and DVDs'. I pulled out my collection of '*Friends*' and watched the entire first season in one day on my computer. It lifted my mood (Joey and Chandler always make me laugh) but my emails continued to pile up unanswered and my real friends went ignored for another day.

If you don't have the luxury of watching an entire season of your favourite sit-com or drama, I can reassure you that there are loads of places throughout the city of Dubai to jump onto a wireless signal and get your work done, either while you're waiting to get connected at home or just while you're out and about.

I think I was probably the last holdout. As I said earlier, I didn't have a 'mobile wireless device' or 'Smart Phone' like a Crackberry or *iPhone* until my husband returned home from a trip to LA after my little *Samsung* died, with an *iPhone4*. I still refuse to get a data package. I really don't need to be connected to my email 24/7 but there are those who do and finding the hotspots is a necessity.

"In our modern, hyper-connected world where information is king and time is always at a premium, the speed of communication can be the difference between success and failure for a business," says David Grunfeld, managing director of *Prose Solutions*. "It's no longer enough to be better than the competition; you have to be faster and more responsive too."

For someone like David, it's a must! So, off to find those hotspots. But once you find one, how do you gain access? It will vary from one place to another. Some are free, others are pay as you go and others are connected to either *Etisalat* or *du*. Are you getting the picture here? I'll say it again… there's not much competition in the telecommunications realm in Dubai. So just pick one or the other and go for it.

As for Wi-Fi access, of course, you're all set if you've purchased a data package but you might want to suspend that when you're in a hotspot to save some money. *Etisalat* has hotspots all over town (www.etisalat.ae/assets/file/Hotspots/userguide/index.html) that you can use with a pre-paid WASL, a GSM post-paid subscription, a credit card or even a hotspot pre-paid card (ranging from AED 15 for one hour to AED 120 for 12 hours). These can be bought on site at the hotspot location. As long as you have an Internet-enabled device, you're good to go.

du has a webpage (www.du.ae/en/wifilocations) where their list of hotspot locations is connected to a Google map so you can easily find them.

There are several locations around town that offer free Wi-Fi as long as you're a paying customer. Some examples include *Caribou Coffee*, *More Café*, Dubai Mall (apparently the entire mall is wired for free Wi-Fi), The Pavilion community centre, *French Connection*, Dubai Airport and assorted hotels. However, reports I've read indicate that some of these free hotspots have connectivity problems.

If you still have a phone with a SIM Card from another country you can access these Wi-Fi hotspots in the same way if you have service (in other words, if you have roaming and are receiving a signal). Just remember, you'll have to pay the roaming charges on top of the Wi-Fi access fees. The other option is to get a visitor's mobile pre-paid package valid for 90 days (non-renewable) if you have an unlocked phone.

The Practicalities

- Passport copy and valid visa (residence or visitor visa) – unless you're just here temporarily and want to pay as you go.

The Five-Step Recap

Step 1

Check the specifications on your mobile phone or laptop to see if they are Internet enabled (there are probably few people on earth other than my mom who don't have both a wireless enabled phone and computer but it would be the first step if you didn't).

Step 2

If you want to access the Internet in a hotspot with your Smart Phone, switch to a local SIM card, as it will be a lot cheaper. If you're not in town for long or your phone happens to be locked from using a foreign SIM card, you can still use your home country phone (as long as you have roaming) and pay as you go using the hot spot pre-paid card (which comes with the access code). For the online subscription option only local credit cards are accepted and it will only send the access code via SMS to a local phone number.

Step 3

If you're here for the long run and haven't already gotten your mobile phone package (as outlined in the last chapter), this would be a good time to do so.

Step 4

Pick a location. Every mall has several hotspots, many hotels, cafés (like *Starbucks*, *Caribou Coffee*, *Second Cup* and *Coffee Bean and Tea Leaf*), phone centres and bookshops. Even on the Metro. Also, check out David's favourites coming up.

Step 5

Search for wireless networks in range, pay the fee and start surfing.

> ## Tip
> As you're traveling around town getting life sorted out and visiting any number of service providers and retail outlets, periodically check to see if there's a wireless signal. You may be lucky enough to find one that's not on the list.

Case Study #1

"In my corporate communications and professional writing business, we collaborate with writers from across the UAE and around the world to develop high quality English and Arabic content for our clients across the region. To effectively manage the constant flow of information that drives my business – and that each one of us now faces in our professional and personal lives – it is vital to have quick and easy access to the web. And as more information is stored in the cloud over the coming years, the need for convenient access to our online information will only increase."

David Grunfeld, managing director, *Prose Solutions*

Over the last few years, Dubai has come a long way in providing Internet access on the go. Here are some of David's favourite hot spots:

- The Shisha Spot: *Tché Tché* – refreshing fresh juices and decent food make this modern shisha café a good choice around Jumeirah Beach Residence.

- The Retro: *Shakespeare & Co.* – tasty meals, pastries and coffee with a number of locations across the city, though the original Sheikh Zayed Road location behind Al Attar Tower still has the best atmosphere.

- The Behemoth: The Dubai Mall – the biggest mall in the world is basically a giant hotspot, so you can connect in any of its many restaurants and public areas… or while ice-skating.

- The Hotel Lobby: *Emirates Towers*, *Grosvenor House*, and several other high-end hotels across the city offer free Wi-Fi; they can be a bit sterile but are ideal for business meetings.

- The Quick Fix: *Starbucks*, *Costa* or many of the other generic coffee shops across the city are Wi-Fi enabled, though some charge an hourly fee to get online.

Case Study #2

"In my role of heading up the team at a Dubai-based management consultancy, my key purpose is to facilitate organisational change. Success is totally dependent upon a positive connection with the management executive I'll be partnering with. As one of my three essential 'filtering meetings' prior to accepting a project, I will always ask to meet the client at The Pavilion, a new and contemporary community and art centre in the heart of downtown. The Pavilion epitomizes business today, portability and scalability, visibility and accessibility, transparent and collaborative, convenient and creative all wrapped together. Grab a coffee, work on a lounge or workspace, hire the theatre, and read in the library. The free and reliable, fast-speed Internet access helps me keep my business rolling along, while I'm cocooned in the most amazingly-creative work space. No need to even have an office."

Debbie Nicol, creator of *embers of the world* and managing director of *business en motion*

The Wrap up

I can't help but revert back to my childhood and my upbringing as a Roman Catholic. A popular scripture (Matthew 7:7) keeps running through my mind and has become a mantra as I wrote this book… *Seek and Ye Shall Find*. It seems a fitting way to end this chapter (or any other chapter of this book for that matter). In Dubai, you can find anything you need. Sometimes you have to dig a bit, ask a lot of questions and park the impatience. There are hundreds of hotspots around town but finding the one that suits your needs, has a consistent, reliable connection and doesn't cost too much, may take a bit of seeking.

Chapter 19

Websites you Need to Know

I was ecstatic in April 2011 when *Google* introduced the 'Panda' (or 'Farmer' depending on who you talk to) that was a new search algorithm that included coding to find websites with quality content. I know that's a pretty subjective term but *Google* decided they needed to take more responsibility for the results its users were getting with searches and, quite honestly, some of the top ranked sites were trash due to somewhat unethical SEO tactics. It's quite controversial but the ultimate goal is to improve the overall quality of the content on the Internet. Pretty tall order, right? And, it's going to take some time.

So, it gives me great pleasure to help you begin your search so you don't have to waste time trudging through the reams and reams of awful sites out there that tout themselves as *the* information site for anything Dubai. Combining my own research, the time I spent in Dubai and the input from survey respondents, I think we can give you a pretty good start.

One of the most popular websites recommended on many of the surveys completed was www.dubizzle.com. It's hailed as *the* place to start when looking to buy or sell anything. From furniture and cars to houses and clothing. It's also a great place to get rid of some stuff when it's time to leave.

"Expat websites like www.expatwoman.com are great for women especially housewives or trailing spouses. *Heels & Deals* (www.heelsanddeals.org) is great for women thinking of starting their own business or for freelancers; and Meetup (www.meetup.com/cities/ae/dubai) has many different types of groups from those of certain nationalities, professions and sports interests," said Canadian Jeanette Todd.

Expat Woman was also popular with Jeanette's fellow Canadian expat, Amy. "There are lots of ladies online who are tapped into various 'grapevines' and who quickly alert the rest of us to various goings-on both serious and gossipy," she shared. Amy also likes GoNabit (www.gonabit.com) as a great source for deals on just about anything.

Here is a collection of other helpful sites that came up in the surveys, during research or in conversation with my expat friends (in alphabetical order):

Ahlan

- www.ahlan.ae
  A popular fashion and lifestyle magazine.

AMEInfo

- www.ameinfo.com
  A news aggregate site focussing on business in the Middle East.

AngloInfo

- http://dubai.angloinfo.com/information.asp#422
  A global expat network that provides solid, well-researched information on essential details about life in Dubai.

Better Homes

- www.bhomes.com
  One of the most commonly recommended real estate companies. It deals with both residential and commercial real estate for both sale and lease.

Cultural Arts Travelogue

- http://culturalartstravelogue.com
  A Middle East based lifestyle website covering culture, arts and travel. The writer reviews various cultural and arts events throughout the region and does interviews with colourful characters.

Crowne Relocation

- www.crownerelo.com
  A relocation company that handles everything from A to Z.

DEWA Locations

- <u>www.dewa.gov.ae/maps/PaymentLocations.aspx#1</u>
  This includes the locations of other services such as
  Etisalat and *Empost*, as well as *ENOC* and *EPPCO*,
  where car emissions tests and registrations are done.

Directory of Business Councils in Dubai

- <u>www.dcci.ae</u>

  Part of Dubai Chamber e-services, this is a
  comprehensive list of all the country-related business
  councils in Dubai with phone numbers and email
  addresses.

Dubai City Guide

- <u>www.dubaicityguide.com</u>

  News, events, entertainment, shopping and
  information for residents.

Dubai Confidential

- <u>www.dubaiconfidential.ae</u>

  Information on the latest trends, fashions, places to
  go and things to do. The writers test out products and
  places and report their experiences to their readers
  along with special offers and vouchers.

Dubai Department of Economic Development (DED)

- www.dubaided.gov.ae/English

  Its mission is to improve e-services, streamline the issuance of licences and simplify the process of doing business in Dubai.

Dubai FAQs

- www.dubaifaqs.com

  Often the site that comes up on the top of search engine rankings when you type in anything related to Dubai.

Dubai Furnished Apartments

- www.dubaifurnishedapartments.com
  Exactly what you'd expect. Focuses on short stay.

Dubai Healthcare City

- www.dhcc.ae

  A web portal that leads to loads of information on the hospitals, clinics and healthcare providers located in Healthcare City. It's a great resource for both practitioners and patients.

Dubai Kidz

- www.dubaikidz.biz

  References and resources on everything kid-related.

Dubai Tourism

- www.dubaitourism.ae
  Good general background information for travel and business visitors and new residents.

Dubizzle

- www.dubizzle.com
  Extensive classified ads.

Emirates Ads

- www.emirates-ads.ae
  It claims to be the UAE's one-stop shop for classifieds but I just happened upon it one day. I haven't tried it and no one else has mentioned it but I think it's worth a look.

ExpatEcho Dubai – Powered by *MoveOne*

- www.expatechodubai.com

- www.moveoneinc.com/blog/category/middle-east/
  A great companion guide to *@Home in Dubai* for expats living in or re-locating to Dubai with regular expat interviews, called *Into Yous*, featuring people like us.

Expat Woman

- www.expatwoman.com
  A resource for expat women (mostly moms) in
  the UAE.

Government of Dubai

- www.dubai.ae
  Official Government of Dubai public portal (comes
  up in Arabic but there's an option on the home page
  to switch to English).

Live, Work, Explore Dubai

- www.explorerpublishing.com/liveworkexplore/dubai
  Great resource for living and working in Dubai
  featuring a regularly updated restaurant guide and
  entertainment venues.

My UAE Guide

- www.myuaeguide.com
  A business and lifestyle guide with extensive
  classified sections.

Offshore HSBC – Expat Explorer Survey

- www.offshore.hsbc.com/1/2/international/expat/expat-survey

  Expat Explorer claims to be "the world's largest global survey of expats". In 2010 there were 4,000 expats who answered questions on finance, quality of life and raising children abroad.

Move – Jet set to a new Home

- http://moveguidesonline.com/movement/#/categories/dubai

  Online chat and advice about moving to a new city.

Property Finder

- http://www.propertyfinder.ae/

  Online classified website, specifically for purchasing or renting properties. It has a search option to find agents and industry news and advice.

Roads and Transport Authority (RTA) Web Portal

- www.rta.ae

  Provides all kinds of information (although not very well laid out) on everything related to Dubai roads, driving, traffic rules and procedures.

Sheikh Mohammed

- www.sheikhmohammed.co.ae

  Official website of Sheikh Mohammed bin Rashid al
  Maktoum, Vice President and Prime Minister of the
  UAE and Ruler of Dubai.

Sheikh Mohammed Centre for Cultural Understanding

- www.cultures.ae

  A great resource for information on the local culture
  and religion.

Silla

- www.silla.ae

  Healthcare portal with written recommendations
  from community members.

Culture & Co.

- www.cultureandcompany.com

  Provides an overview of Dubai culture and history
  and offers cultural assimilation courses, cultural
  tours and other programs.

UAE Interact

- www.uaeinteract.com
  Has an awesome interactive map of Dubai.

United Arab Emirates Ministry of Economy

- http://www.economy.ae
  An online investor's guide to the UAE.

Wills UAE

- http://willsuae.com
  A law firm in the UAE licensed to write wills and provide succession planning.

General Expat Advice

EBooks for Expats

- http://ebooks.escapeartist.com/index.php
  A collection of expat ebooks covering topics from offshore investing to overseas employment.

Expat Daily News

- http://www.expatdailynews.com
  A news portal and forum on expat living.

Expat Bookshop

- www.expatbookshop.com
  The place to go to find books by and for people who live abroad.

The Expat Coach Directory

- www.theexpatcoachdirectory.com
  A listing of life coaches who specialise in expat-related issues.

Expat Financial Questions Answered (FQA)

- www.expatfqa.com
  Financial advice for expatriates by a team of financial advisors and wealth managers.

Expat Women

- www.expatwomen.com
  The largest global website with resources for expatriate women around the world featuring readers' stories, expat women blogs, interviews, motivational messages and inspirational newsletter.

Success Abroad Coaching

- http://successabroadcoaching.com
  Advice and guidance for people considering a move abroad.

The Practicalities

You'll need:

- An Internet enabled computer or mobile computing device.

- Internet access at home or a comfy Internet café, hotel lobby or shopping mall.

- Your handy list of 'Websites you Need to Know' from *@Home in Dubai*.

The Five-Step Recap

Step 1

Get advice on websites to check out from trusted friends and sources.

Step 2

Peruse the list included in this chapter and note other websites interspersed throughout the book (see list compiled in *Resource Section*).

Step 3

You'll probably have a huge list so visit them in some type of orderly fashion (unless you have all day to spend). You should have a To Do list a mile long by now so see if there are any sites that will help you tick a few of those off.

Step 4

Grab a notebook or open a memo, word document or note page on your Internet cruising device of choice.

Step 5

Take notes as you come across any great advice, contact information or tip on accomplishing some of the goals you've listed and bookmark any sites you want to visit regularly.

Tip

"I meet many people who moved to Dubai based purely on the information they were given/read/heard. I would recommend everyone to actually visit before making any decision."

Bijay Shah, national director, *BNI Middle East*

Case Study #1

"When you research anything, get three opinions (because facts do differ). Some of the websites are old or out-dated, so also speak to people who have lived here for many years. Their advice will be invaluable."

Gillian from South Africa

Case Study #2

"I get almost all of my news online (<u>cbc.ca</u> all the way). Also the *CNN*, *BBC* and the *Economist* websites. I check *Gulf News* online only if I want the government perspective. Increasingly, I check *Al Jazeera's* English website."

Amy, Canadian

The Wrap Up

Along with the online local newspapers the most common reply on favourite websites on the surveys was *Twitter* and blogs. If you use *Twitter*, just type in #MovingtoDubai in the search and you'll get a long list of people and advice. It's a great place to post queries as well. But don't count on it for everything. A word of caution: you can spend hours and days reading through online resources and references and never get anything done. At one stage you'll just have to believe you've done all the research you need and then it's time for 'boots on the ground' as my husband says.

Chapter 20

Local Forums

If you can find a group, online or offline, where you can connect on a common interest or passion and have an opportunity to share ideas and ask questions, it's a great way to get settled into life in Dubai. My favourite place to chat online with fellow professionals is *LinkedIn* (www.linkedin.com). There's a litany of groups so do a categorical search and pick one that matches your interests. My favourites are Freelance Web Writers, Freelance Writers Connection and Writer's Showcase. There are locally based groups as well that have online discussions and meet in person too.

"One lonely night while Chris was off flying or training, and I was pinging off the walls of my nearly-bare apartment, I posted that I was a newcomer on *Expat Woman*. I received a bunch of lovely, encouraging messages, including one from a lady who lived in the same building and who asked if I wanted to meet for coffee. It was through that connection that I met some of my dearest friends in Dubai," says Amy from Canada.

I would also consider *Facebook* a kind of forum. There are tons of Dubai-based groups that have discussions on a wide variety of topics. I actually started and manage a group called 'Expats Living in Dubai'. Sometimes people will post items for sale and apartments to rent but it's not as prolific as *Dubizzle* yet. Sometimes someone who is new in town will just reach out to see if anyone wants to get together for coffee, like Amy's new friend on *Expat Woman* did.

Dubai Forums (www.dubaiforums.com) is another good place to start. On the homepage, there's a list of a wide variety of forums addressing subjects from philosophy and religion to romance and employment. The forums fall under eight categories:

- Dubai Discussions

- Dubai Employment

- Dubai Expat Forums

- Dubai Consumer

- Dubai Business

- Dubai Tech Discussions

- Dubai Culture

- Private Places on Dubai Forums

Other popular forums:

Allo Expat

* www.alloexpat.com/dubai_expat_forum
  Online community resources and forums for Dubai expats.

Dubai Dad's Club

* www.dubaidadsclub.com
  An online social network for dads in Dubai.

EmiratesMac

* www.emiratesmac.com
  This forum is specifically for Mac users (I'm a recent convert so I may just check it out). You can ask other users questions or provide tips yourself. You can even buy and sell things.

Expat Forum – Dubai

* www.expatforum.com
  (click on the Dubai flag at the top... it's easier than including the direct link)
  This one's an online forum for expats living in Dubai (of course) who wish to discuss food, meet friends, talk Dubai property, finances and jobs.

Meetup Dubai

- www.meetup.com/cities/ae/dubai
  There are 141 Meetup groups in and around Dubai
  that meet in person in great venues all around town.
  It's an opportunity to scout out different parts of
  town and meet new people at the same time. Topics
  range from books and wine to writing and theatre.
  There are business-related groups, meditation groups
  and even a group to help out new iPhone users.

TEDx Dubai

- http://tedxdubai.com
  TEDx is a program of local, independently
  organised forums that bring people together to hear
  inspirational speakers and to share in the global TED
  movement. Individuals in several Emirates have
  created annual TED events.

UAE Forum – Desert Speak

- www.desertspeak.com
  This forum includes discussion groups such as:
  Residents and Visitors, Education in the UAE,
  Events in the UAE, Property in the UAE, UAE
  Classifieds and Dubai Sandbox (pages that don't fit
  anywhere else).

The Practicalities

You'll need:

- Internet access to do the search and review your options.

- An interest in spreading your wings and meeting new people.

- Courage to walk into a room of strangers (who just might become friends) or join an online discussion.

The Five-Step Recap

Step 1

Ask around for suggestions on forums in which you may be interested.

Step 2

Review the list provided here.

Step 3

Jump into a discussion that grabs your attention or see when the next meeting is scheduled.

Step 4

Put it on your calendar (it'll feel great).

Step 5

Attend an 'on the ground' meeting or engage in a conversation with a fellow forum member.

Tip

"Do your advance research. Talk to as many people as possible. Spend time networking and meeting new people. Try and get to know the locals. They are truly lovely people, remember this is their country and they are more approachable and welcoming than you might imagine."

Eithne Treanor, managing director, *E. Treanor Media*

Case Study #1

"There are many local forums that revolve around different themes and give participants the opportunity to interact and share ideas. I have joined 'The Law of Attraction' Meetup group. I get regular updates on monthly meetings, location, guest speaker and all the relevant details. Saves me from having to go and search for it. Another great reason I love Meetup is that you can rate the speakers and see who else will be attending and initiate a conversation online before you meet in person. This forum is well worth investigating. The online interface is amazing and the in-person meetings have been productive for me both personally and professionally. I had the opportunity to be the guest speaker at one meeting and it resulted in four follow up appointments, a coaching client who signed up and an invitation to be interviewed on TV. I sold 20 books and have a video of my presentation I can use on my website. I also recently joined the TEDx Dubai face-to-face gathering held at the World Trade Centre. What a fabulous and eclectic conglomeration of minds, ideas and approaches. I highly recommend joining the lottery for free tickets when they are announced."

Debbie Nicol, creator of *embers of the world* and managing director, *business en motion*

Case Study #2

"Dubai Knowledge Village (DKV) regularly organises a series of Breakfast Club gatherings, at least once a quarter. I have moderated several of these lively, engaging and informative panels. We have discussed issues in the work place, how locals and expats interact, also the state of human resources in the city and a recent panel on labour laws brought the discussion around to fairness, workers rights and where the expat stands in relation to 'Emiratisation' of the city and country in key job areas. I moderated an extremely lively session on entrepreneurship and the support in place for locals and expats. An open and frank discussion about issues, problems, ideas and solutions has always been encouraged with an interactive and lively debate guaranteed. DKV then presents a report of these findings to the government office."

Eithne Treanor, managing director, *E. Treanor Media*

The Wrap Up

As I see it, forums are less formal, loose discussions (and sometimes ranting and ramblings) on any topic under the sun. It reminds me of those community (or city hall) meetings where people come to discuss an issue of common concern or air their grievances. Sometimes you can come away with some valuable input and other times you may leave the conversation more confused that ever before. The best approach is to include a resource like this in the mix of social interaction options, professional organisations or groups.

Chapter 21

Bloggers and Tweeters to Follow

There's a whole slew of Tweeters and bloggers out there talking about day-to-day life in Dubai highlighting everything from the touristy stuff to culinary adventures and a few that like to have a rant now and then.

Some great (yet controversial) blogs like www.secretdubaidiary.blogspot.com, who also started the *UAE Community Blogs* (http://uaecommunity.blogspot.com), get blocked every once in a while so make sure you check them out before you get here or try accessing through a virtual private network (VPN). If you are a blogger in Dubai you do have to mind your manners as blogger and activist Ahmed Mansour discovered when he was arrested in April 2011. According to Reuters the official charge was possession of alcohol but various news reports claim he was arrested for calling for free elections and reforms.

"There are a lot of great blogs – *Fake Plastic Souks*, *Life In Dubai*, *The UAE Community Blog*," says Susan Castle from Scotland (who also blogs at http://susanthecoach.wordpress.com, usually about personal and business development but often about living in Dubai as well).

One of my personal favourites is *Arabian Tales and Other Amazing Adventures* by American expat, Katie Foster. She has a refreshingly positive view of life in Dubai. She started blogging shortly after she and her husband arrived in 2010 and she deftly brings you along on her wide-eyed discoveries of a new part of the world. Her almost child-like glee is infectious (and since she's a grandmother, it's refreshing to see someone so open to new experiences… this is the first time she's lived outside her hometown of Fort Lauderdale, Florida). Her blog on the 'Top 10 Reasons I Love Living in Dubai!' is fabulous. Re-printed with her permission, here are the first three:

1) **You can get ANYTHING delivered** at any hour, night or day: food, cosmetics, office supplies, dry cleaning, rental cars… Burger King at 3 am? No problem!

2) **I embraced the Electronic Age** and went completely paperless and now conduct all my business on the Internet. It feels good doing my part to save the trees and the planet.

3) **The opportunity to pray five times a day with our Muslim friends** as the call to prayer begins at 4:40 am and can be heard in every corner of Dubai five times a day. I now say my own prayer for peace at these calls to prayer as just a small gesture of solidarity with my Muslim friends.

… you'll have to visit her blog to see the rest but be prepared to take some time because you won't be able to stop at one.

So, grab a cup of tea or coffee, put your feet up and enjoy! This is by no means an exhaustive list of bloggers in Dubai (more come on line every day) but it's a good start.

Bloggers (in alphabetical order)

An Englishman in Dubai

- http://englishmanindubai.com
  For a little more testosterone this is one Englishman's "Little Blog about Life as an Expat in Dubai".

Arabian Tales and Other Amazing Adventures

- http://arabiantalesandotheramazingadventures. blogspot.com
  Written by American expat, good friend and freelance writer Katie Foster. She invites other expats to guest blog about their experiences.

Arabic Zeal

- www.arabiczeal.com
  Written by Holly Warah, who also Tweets @dubai_ words. She includes loads of great photos as well.

"Arabic Zeal explores the books, food and culture of the region. Discover recommended reading for Westerners: novels, memoirs and nonfiction that shed light on the Arab World".

Adventures in Dubailand

- www.pamelarollings.blogspot.com
  Pam has not been blogging much lately but there's still some great information from her perspective on living in Dubai and she did provide some fresh advice for us in her *@Home in Dubai* survey.

Dubai Bites

- http://dubai-bites.com
  Recipes, musings and culinary adventures. I'm not a foodie but my Dubai foodie friends love this blog and I have to admit, it had my mouth watering.

Dubai Confidential

- www.dubaiconfidential.ae
  "Hidden Gems of Dubai" was founded in April 2011 and after a few short months already had 600 subscribers and 25,000 page hits (must have something going for it). They even have a film club.

Dubai Days

- http://dubaidays-dubaidaisy.blogspot.com
  "An Englishwoman unexpectedly living a life of
  leisure in Dubai while my wonderful long-suffering
  husband works his socks off". She also Tweets @
  dubaidays.

Fake Plastic Souks

- http://fakeplasticsouks.blogspot.com
  Written by blogger Alexander McNabb who also
  organises Geek Fest in locations throughout the
  Middle East.

The Hedonista

- www.thehedonista.com
  An Aussie named Sarah Walton who blogs about
  "Living a life of pleasure… food, wine, sunshine,
  with the occasional pipe… of shisha". There's a
  section on her blog called Dubai-Ified. She also
  Tweets @the_hedonista.

Life in Dubai

- www.dubaithoughts.blogspot.com
  A great walk through time by an Australian who
  lived in Dubai from 1977-1984 and then moved back
  in 2005.

Longhorns and Camels

- http://longhornsandcamels.wordpress.com
  One of my favourites, as Lynda Skok Martinez
  shares honest and open insight into everything from
  hired help to the Emirati wedding she crashed. She
  includes some awesome photography as well.

Sandier Pastures

- www.sandierpastures.com
  "Desert Living Dubai Style". Grace also tweets @
  sandierpastures.

Scribblelicious

- www.scribblelicious.com
  Here's another one for foodies. Great (affordable)
  restaurant reviews and food photos that make your
  mouth water. It's also peppered with bits of advice
  on other aspects of Dubai living too!

Sleepless in Dubai

- http://zvezdanarashkovich.webs.com/apps/blog
  Written by Svezdana Rashkovich, blogger and
  author of a novel called *Dubai Wives*. Her blog talks
  about her life as an expat, (which she started as a
  TCK), mom to four TCK's and wife to a Sudanese/
  Egyptian. In her words she's "Trying to do it
  all in high heels while navigating sand, traffic, the
  joys of multi-cultural as well as the quirky but
  fabulous fellow Dubaians".

TexPat Faith

- http://texpatfaith.wordpress.com/about
  Expat adventures through the eyes of faith by Texan
  (transplanted from Virginia) Shirley W Ralston.
  Shirley's a new blogger and takes a real unique look
  at expat life in Dubai.

UAE Community Blog

- www.uaecommunity.blogspot.com
  Highlights a wide selection of other bloggers in
  Dubai.

Dubai-Based Tweeters

Descriptions are their *Twitter* profiles)

@akankshaGoel

Partner at Socialize.ae. Marketing insider and trainer lurking around dubious Dubai. Ex-Editor of STUFF Magazine, Singapore. Likes all things shiny that beep.

* http://www.socialize.ae

@Catboy_Dubai (radio personality)

Too fat for fashion.

* http://dubai92.com

@dubaiinformer

Dubai News and UAE updates from A to Z.

* http://dubaiinformer.com/

@dubai_ladies

Updates for the women, mums and young ladies in Dubai – News/Events/Offers etc.

@DXBMediaOffice

The official *Twitter* feed from the Government of Dubai Media Office. Tweets are in both Arabic and English.

@ExpatWomanDubai

Features, advice, a busy forum, job ads, classifieds, competitions, events and more – Dubai, Qatar and Abu Dhabi.

* http://www.expatwoman.com/Dubai

@farrukhnaeem

English advertising copywriter, SEO expert, journalist, blogger and cartoon addict.

* http://www.farrukhnaeem.com

@GeekFestDubai

The offline social for online socialisers and a *Twitterfeed* of all things geeky.

* http://www.shelter.ae

@geordiearmani

A mad Geordie, based in Dubai, mother to a seven-year-old and five adorable kitties. Social Networking Queen.

* http://www.geordiearmani.com

@LifeinUAE

News and updates on Dubai.

* http://wefollow.com/LifeinUAE

@property_finder

Propertyfinder is the number one dedicated property portal in the UAE.

- http://www.propertyfinder.ae

@rania711

I'm an online marketing and social media advocate. I tweet my opinion and whatever gets my attention and matters to me.

- http://www.facebook.com/rania711

@susanthecoach

Susan Castle founded Outwith The Dots Success Coaching to empower people to live rich and wonderful lives with unconventional wisdom.

- http://www.Outwiththedots.com

@thatdubaiguy

Management at Restaurant/Ultra-Lounge @carameldubai in DIFC, Dubai.

- http://www.caramelgroup.com

@TimeOutDubai

Time Out Dubai magazine.

* http://www.timeoutdubai.com

@UAEHashtags (was fairly new when this was written so keep watching)

We are here to keep you updated with all that's happening in the UAE on the spot. To people, by people! Follow us to stay updated!

Tip

If you want to follow Dubai Tweeters you'll have to set up a profile on *Twitter*. Go to www.twitter.com, fill in your name, email and choose a password and click on *Join*. Truly as easy as 1-2-3.

The Wrap Up

I would probably be remiss if I didn't include my *Twitter* handle and blog. It's not always specific to Dubai but occasionally I'll talk about the life and times of a freelance writer living as an expat. On *Twitter* I'm @AnnetheWriter (go figure) and my blog is www.anne-writingjustbecause. bogspot.com. Comments are most welcome!

If you're bored and looking for something to do once you've moved into your new place; your phone is hooked up and your Internet is connected; you've gotten your driving licence and bought your car; why not start a blog? It's just another way to connect to a like-minded online community. Blogger (www.blogspot.com) and Wordpress (www.wordpress.com) are the most popular platforms.

Chapter 22

Online Shopping and Deliveries

The term 'shopping' has taken on a whole new meaning in Dubai. It's even one of the main tourist attractions. I guess it's understandable when one mall has a ski hill and another one has the biggest fish tank in the world and a skating rink.

When my mom and two sisters visited me in February of the first year I was here, I thought I would take them on the '*Big Bus*' tour. My sister, Sue, and I had done one in London and had a blast. Of the four of us, only one is a shopper so we don't tend to spend much time in malls when we're together. A word of advice... don't do the Beach Tour option of the '*Big Bus*' tour unless you're an avid shopper. That particular route stops at no less than six malls (they've probably added a few more since then as they just keep on building them).

Seriously, we boarded at Souk Madinat and then stopped at Mall of the Emirates, Dubai Mall, Wafi Centre, Deira City Centre and the Burjuman Mall. I just wanted to see the Dubai Museum but we would have had to jump on the next line (the City Tour) at Burjuman, but didn't have time to get there and back to our original stop (where the car was parked) before our ticket ran out. It wasn't a total loss. We did see *Atlantis* and the *Burj Al Arab*.

If I have to shop, I'd rather do it from the comfort of my own home and Dubai hasn't missed a shopping beat with that either. If you're a shopper, you'll love both the on the ground and online shopping that abounds in Dubai. My vote goes to the online variety as it saves time and you don't have to fight the traffic and try to find parking.

Popular Online Shopping Sites

If you're a techno geek, I've heard that *Emirates Avenue* (<u>www.emiratesavenue.com</u>) is great. It calls itself the number one online electronics store in the UAE. If you follow *Emirates Avenue* on *Twitter* or *Facebook*, you get regular coupons and updates. Their payment policy is cash on delivery (COD) or bank transfer. This seems to be most common with Dubai online shopping sites, as it's difficult to establish a system for online payment according to an article in *The National*, 'UAE online shopping stalled', published on May 17, 2011.

The article claims, "A lack of online payment providers could be holding back the development of web shopping in the Emirates". From what I see and hear, people are happily shopping and ordering online at a great rate. An article talking about the results of a survey *MasterCard* conducted supports my hypothesis.

"The percentage of respondents who access Internet to do their shopping grew from 29 per cent in 2009 to 42 per cent, according the findings of a study on online shopping by *MasterCard*", according to a *Khaleej Times* (www. khaleejtimes.com) article titled 'Online shopping gains more currency in UAE', on March 18, 2011.

I don't think the online payment issue is slowing things down. Most people feel that COD is preferable anyways. That way you know you'll get your goods before you spend the money and some shady, fake web-front isn't going to make off with your money, without making good on your order.

Another popular site for electronics is *Spend Wisor* (www. spendwisor.com). They'll do *PayPal* as well as COD or credit card (on delivery) and it's free delivery for orders over AED 200 within the UAE.

For your basic big box store, *Carrefour* has an extensive online shopping website at www.ic4UAE.com. It's probably one of the ones you can trust, as it's a well-known, established department store. They offer free delivery on large items to anywhere in the UAE… smaller items are delivered by UPS.

Take out and delivery has also been taken to greater heights, along with all the skyscrapers, in Dubai. Most restaurants have online menus and delivery. Even *Burger King* and *McDonalds* will deliver! No more sending dad out to pick up burgers for dinner.

Here are a few other online shopping sites to whet your appetite:

- www.aido.com has kids' stuff, gift ideas, books, DVDs and electronics. Note: the company is based in Dubai but prices are quoted in dollars because they distribute worldwide.

- www.alshop.com is a great site to shop for electronics.

- www.burjmall.com has everything from electronics to clothing.

- www.quickdubai.com even includes a currency converter.

- www.souq.com has pretty much everything... cars, jewellery, furniture, toys, electronics and a 'Deal of the Day' to keep you coming back.

- www.sukar.com is an exclusive shopping club.

The Online Coupon Movement

Now that you've found all the shopping you can possibly cope with, it's time to get your 'group on' and get some deals. Group buying is all the rage in Dubai and has become a powerful online marketing tool for retailers to feature their products online.

"One-day deals, offered online, have caught the interest of buyers of all ages and, it is a virtual race against the clock before the offer expires", according to an article in *The Intelligent SME* (www.theintelligentsme.com) titled 'Deal of the Day'. It combines the joy of shopping with the competitive spirit. The deals range from hotel packages and electronics to spa discounts, *Ferrari World* passes and even cars. UAE based *Cobone* has actually sold several *Nissan* Pathfinders at a discount online.

"I have used three online coupon services (cobone.com, gonabit.com and groupon.com) and all coupons were delivered by email. The coupons are at least 50% off or sometimes even more," said Katie Foster, American blogger and freelance writer. "I have only had one 'dog' – a three-hour yacht cruise and BBQ (the cruise only consisted of a trip from Dubai Marina to *Atlantis* and back – about an hour – then we moored in the little basin outside the Marine Centre and ate terrible food while we sweated. Had I paid full price I probably would have sunk the boat)."

Hopefully Groupon will still be around since financial information was released illegally during the IPO process in August 2011. We'll see!

Other online deal sites highlighted in *The Intelligent SME* article included www.yallabanada.com and www.arabianoffer.com.

Practicalities

- You'll need a computer or Smart Phone with Internet access and a passion for hunting down a great deal.

Five-Step Recap

Step 1

Make your shopping list.

Step 2

Review the list of sites to see who carries what you need.

Step 3

Compare prices.

Step 4

Join the coupon sites and check to see if they're offering any deals on the item you need.

Step 5

Order your stuff and sit back and wait for it to be delivered.

Case Study #1

"I am a big fan of online shopping! Dubai is a place that is filled with large malls with anything and everything your heart desires, however if you happen to be shop and crowd averse its good to have options. I also shop online for talent and services, which has proven to be very efficient and cost effective. I personally find the following sites have made a big difference to my shopping habits:

1. www.Amazon.com – Deliveries to Dubai are fairly easy and reliable. I have ordered books and DVDs regularly from *Amazon* (there's no home delivery so you'll need a PO Box... see *Chapter 6 Water, Electricity (DEWA), Gas... and Mail Delivery*).

2. www.mycroburst.com – I have used *Mycroburst* when designing both of my company logos and for designing business cards and stationery. I love this site! You create a profile and fill a brief on what you need. You then put up an amount of money you are willing to pay for the job. Throughout the week you will receive designs from all over

the world; much more efficient and much more choice than going to a graphic designer. For *Ti22 Films* I received 78 designs and for *Bambootique* I received 98 designs and I am very happy with my final logos.

3. I have used a number of websites to hire individuals and virtual assistants to carry out tasks for me online. Sites include: www.odesk. com, www.elance.com and www.tryasksunday. com. All have been useful and have saved me time. A Dubai-based VA company has just been launched, Platinum VA, I am looking forward to trying them.

4. All of my holidays are planned and booked online. Why go to a travel agent when in a few clicks I can receive my confirmation email? I recommend www.expedia.com and have booked flights directly through a number of airlines online. It's much more time efficient.

5. I order flowers online every year for family member birthdays and occasions. I have been using an international site but am considering www.flowers.ae.

6. I book tickets for all events and concerts online. I have had good experiences booking on www. timeouttickets.com, the *Madinat Theatre* (www. madinattheatre.com) website as well as for one off

events such as Emirates Literature festival (www. eaifl.com), and would recommend this.

7. If a popular movie opens in the cinema, I book tickets in advance on <u>www.grandcinemas.com</u>.

Reim el Houni, producer/managing director of *Ti22 Films* and managing director of *Bambootique*

Case Study #2

"I spend hours online everyday testing the boundaries of the Internet, making millions of conscious and unconscious impressions. Each time I find an unknown digital gem, the nerdy kid inside me giggles as I share it with my social network. It's like finding little presents and uncovering precious needles in an ever-expanding haystack. I realize that most people do not share my geeky joy (my clients definitely do not), so to them I often say: 'Why not go to online sites where you KNOW your gifts will be'? The truth is that online shopping in the Middle East still has a long way to go in order to match the businesses that are currently booming online. One of the primary reasons for this is the fact that most people do not trust the sites enough to surrender their credit card information. Another reason is the fear that the package may get lost in the mail. Given these obstacles, I feel that we, the digital community, should give credit and encourage local companies that do sell their products online and offer reliable services. Instead of shying away from online shopping in the MENA region, we should be encouraging the growth of online industries. In response to this, I decided to troll the net for a few Dubai online shopping sites that are reliable and have given me GREAT service... www.nahel.com, www.foodonclick.com and www.nextlevelracing.ae.

(Re-printed from *Interactive Middle East* with permission from the author, Reem Hameed, digital media strategist and small business consultant, www.reemhameed.com)

The Wrap up

When doing your online shopping you don't have to be limited to websites based in Dubai. We used a great service offered by *Aramex* called Shop and Ship (www.shopandship.com). You can use a *MasterCard* or pay COD and can purchase from sites in the US, UK and Europe. We usually ordered from the US and our goods were delivered to the *Aramex* facility in New York and then delivered to our doorstep in Dubai. I must add a caveat here. Websites and businesses in Dubai come and go quite frequently. Many online businesses are start-ups and may or may not make the cut. Most of the sites recommended have been around for a while but you just never know.

Chapter 23

Connecting – Face-to-Face

Professional Networks

In the book *Expat Women Confessions: 50 Answers to your Real-Life Questions about Living Abroad* (<u>www.expatwomen.com</u>) there is a great piece of advice about local groups and networks. "If you don't find a group, network or association that interests you, do not be afraid to set one up yourself," say the authors, Andrea Martin and Victoria Hepworth.

I actually did this with both a charity-oriented group and a writer's circle. As we were planning our move to Dubai I read a book, *Leaving Microsoft to Change the World*, about an ex-Microsoft exec who changed his life around by starting a charity called Room to Read. I was so impressed by the organisation that I started the Dubai volunteer chapter along with a new friend I met who had been involved with the organisation in Hong Kong. Two years later I was sitting around with a group of friends and we were all talking about 'when I write my book'.

I decided to hold everyone to their word (including me) and started a group that meets monthly called Flamingo Authors (since I lived in a compound called 'Flamingo Villas' and we had the first meeting at my place I thought it was appropriate).

Now, not everyone has the kind of drive (or even interest) it takes to lead the charge, so there are loads of networks that already exist. There's bound to be one that appeals to you.

"For newcomers who have their own business or for those who are thinking about starting their own business I would of course recommend *Heels & Deals*," says British expat, Claire Fenner, co-founder of the organisation. "I would also recommend business groups such as the British Business Group and other national business groups. There are many other networks such as the American Women's Association."

Claire's not the only one to recommend *Heels & Deals* (but she's a bit biased, right?). "*Heels & Deals* is great for meeting other women in business, *BNI (Business Networking International)* is also great for business if you're prepared to commit to 5 am starts once a week," said Susan Castle, founder of *Outwith the Dots* and an expat from Scotland. "I also highly recommend *The Referral Institute* run by Phil Bedford if you're planning to do business in Dubai," says Susan. "It not only provides extensive training to help build referral business but is also great for networking with fellow entrepreneurs and potential clients."

"*Heels & Deals* is awesome for females with an entrepreneurial streak. In Dubai there is pretty much a group for every interest: sports groups, choirs and law of attraction groups," says Brit, Karen Beggs from Northern Ireland.

I may have started a writing group but there are several in Dubai that already existed (like the *Meetup* for writers). They just didn't meet my needs at the time.

"The writing groups I joined recently are immensely enjoyable and a place where you meet like-minded people. Also, professional organisations like TESOLArabia (for teachers) are great for professional development," said Padmini Sankar, a long-time Indian expat (and a member of Flamingo Authors).

If you're hunting for the perfect group there are plenty of sources. "*TimeOut* (great source for everything around town for the whole family), *What's On* (similar to *Time Out*, but with wider focus), *The Dubai Explorer* (great book to get you started), www.expatwoman.com (for events/meeting others and for advice regarding anything on their forum), and www.heelsanddeals.org (for networking)," says Dhuha, a British-Yemini.

Once you get out and start meeting people who share the same profession as you do, you'll often find some you click with on other levels too.

"Some of the very good friends I've made here and who are still friends are people I met at these organised networking groups when I first came to Dubai," said Fiona Thomas, a marketing specialist from Scotland.

There's tons of advice out there on how to assimilate into your new culture and one suggestion is to try to mix with the locals, which isn't particularly easy in Dubai. It is good advice, but don't disregard the opportunities to interact with your fellow home countrymen as well.

"The nationality based organisations are generally good – I found the Irish Business Network hugely helpful," said Dawn from (where else?) Ireland.

Other professional networking groups recommended include:

- American Business Council of Dubai and the Northern Emirates, www.abcdubai.com

- Arab Business Club, www.arabbusinessclub.com

- *BNI – Business Networking International*, www. bni.com, click on 'Find a Chapter' and go to United Arab Emirates.

- British Business Group, www.britbiz-uae.com

- Canadian Business Council, www.cbc-dubai.com

- Danes in Dubai, www.danesindubai.com, includes Danish Business Council and Danish Business Women in Dubai, a wonderful group of women for which I actually did a writing workshop.

- Dubai Chamber of Commerce and Industry, www.dubaichamber.com

- International Business Women's Group (IBWG), www.ibwgdubai.com

- InterNations, www.internations.org/dubai-expats

- Irish Business Network Dubai, www.irishsocietydubai.com

- Toast Masters Dubai Chapter, www.dubaitoastmasters.org

The Practicalities

- If you're going to attend networking events and take part in professional seminars and workshops, might as well get a business card... at least with your name, mobile number and email address.

- Have an idea in mind of what you want to accomplish at each event, even if it's just to make some preliminary contacts and inquiries. Be prepared to answer the question: What do you do?

The Five-Step Recap

Step 1

Review the recommended professional organisations, start a list of those that meet your criteria and prioritize. That is, after you establish your criteria.

Step 2

Visit the websites to learn more about each organisation and see when the next meeting is scheduled.

Step 3

Contact the organisation to find out what the requirements for membership are and if you can attend as a guest for the first couple of times. Don't join until you've scoped out the group and determined whether or not it suits you and your needs.

Step 4

Put the next meeting on your calendar.

Step 5

Practice your elevator speech (in answer to that ubiquitous question – What do you do?).

Case Study #1

"I have attended nearly every possible group and social networking organisation possible in the UAE. For women entrepreneurs: *Heels & Deals* and *Woman2Woman*; for businesses: *BNI (Business Network International)* and Rotary Club; for referral marketing: Certified Networkers through *The Referral Institute*; Abu Dhabi Networking group and *Toastmasters*. For newcomers I would advise that they try whatever they feel is the best for their business or as a way of plugging into the social scene."

Preethi Janice D'Sa (Jan), Indian expat and freelance writer

Case Study #2

"I joined the Australian Business Council and it was a great place to meet with other Aussies at social events, reminisce about home, and network. I ended up on the executive committee as a volunteer because I saw how much value the council provided to both businesses and individuals. I also joined *Heels & Deals*, a women's entrepreneur group which was a lovely environment to make new friends and network for business purposes."

Kara Boden, Australian

The Wrap Up

Professional networking has become almost cult-like in Dubai. Practically everyone I know has joined a *BNI* group (there are at least 10 in various locations throughout the city) and every other person I talk to has taken one or more of Phil Bedford's certified networking courses at *The Referral Institute*. If you have the time, money and patience, it's worth looking into as I've heard some great success stories. I've met Phil a couple of times and I like his philosophy on work and life. However, if you're already a skilled networker and know how to work a room, just get out there and meet some people!

Chapter 24

Clubs – Social/Volunteer/Sport

Social

I know this is going to sound like the fifth call to prayer of the day but I'm going to repeat... Dubai is not like any other expat assignment you'll find anywhere else in the world. Again, due to the expat-intense fabric of the populace, there's plenty of socialising going on and it's not hard to find. You just have to stop, look and listen. I know sometimes that's easier said than done. The advice comes easily after living there almost four years. British expat Claire Fenner felt the same way.

"When I first moved here in 1997 my biggest challenge was probably meeting people socially outside of work. My husband had moved here almost a year before me so he already had a social circle established when I arrived but I also wanted to meet different people," said Claire. "This happened over time and when we moved back here in 2002 from Hong Kong I felt a lot more confident when meeting new people and started making more friends."

Several people recommend *Expat Woman* coffee mornings that are held weekly in various locations from one end of Dubai to the other. Visit the website at <u>www.expatwoman.com</u> just to check days and times as more locations are added and times do vary.

The best advice that came through loud and clear from all survey respondents is to try to experience a variety of groups. I would suggest beginning your environmental assimilation with the local culture by visiting the Jumeirah Mosque (the only mosque in Dubai open to non-Muslims). Take the tour and experience the 'A Taste of the Emirates: Open Doors. Open Minds' program. It's quite an eye-opener (<u>www.cultures.ae/jumeirah_mosque_visit.php</u>).

"I would like to recommend the Sheik Mohammad Centre for Cultural Understanding. Also, I think all newcomers in Dubai should visit the local museum and the big Mosque. In my opinion that's the least you can do when you come to the UAE. Try to get to know the culture, understand Islam and always show respect," said Danish expat, Vibeke Nurgberg.

I have to admit that I didn't visit the mosque until much later in my Dubai experience but wish I had done it sooner. One of my first experiences with a social club was the American Women's Association (AWA, <u>www.awadubai.org</u>), staying well within my comfort zone. It's a very active group and has programs year-round. It even began a Koran education program in the spring of 2011 that has become popular. During the summer when half the city empties, escaping the soaring temperatures, the Summer Gals program kicks in and includes luncheons, shopping trips (to great spots like the Blue Souk), wine tastings and bowling. Or, anything a member decides they want to organise.

"You have to open yourself to all opportunities to get out and meet others, ask questions and be open to new experiences," says American expat, W Mervis, who was my personal saviour when I first moved to Dubai and the person who took me to my first AWA Meet 'n' Greet.

If you're not the 'lunch and learn' type, you could join a social club that revolves around a hobby or specific activity.

"Dubai is a great place for hobbies and I would strongly recommend anyone moving here to take something up. I took up salsa (dancing) and it proved fantastic in terms of making a new group of friends. It's very social by nature," says Brit, Karen Osman.

As expats, we're a pretty friendly group and you may just luck into a neighbour like mine to take you under his or her wing. We were blessed to not only have great neighbours but also knew a few people already living in Dubai. Take advantage of those contacts if at all possible like Italian expat Alba Micheli Geddes and I did.

"I was lucky I already had friends here who gave me the lowdown on everything. From time to time I turned to www.expatwoman.com to get other people's perspectives and advice on small issues," Alba said.

Others turn to some of the popular lifestyle magazines found in practically every shop in Dubai and also online.

"There are a multitude of activities in Dubai. I found the best way to find something that was of interest to me was to look in the *Connector Magazine* (http://mydubaiconnection.com) or *Time Out* (www.timeoutdubai.com)," says British/Canadian expat Tia DeBenedictis. "Hang in there. It's hard at first but get involved in as many activities as you can before you pick and choose what is right for you," says Tia. "There is a lot to do so make it your mission to learn something new every month."

Other recommended organisations:

- ANZA – for Australians and New Zealanders living in Dubai, www.anzauae.org

- Dubai Caledonian Society, www.dubaicaledoniansociety.com

- Dubai Community Theatre and Arts Centre (DUCTAC), www.ductac.org

- Dubai Irish Society, www.irishindubai.com

- Dubai Ladies Club, www.dubailadiesclub.com

- Dubai Natural History Group,
  www.enhg.org/dubai/dubai.htm

- SolidariTea Arabia,
  www.facebook.com/Solidaritea

Volunteering

Since the summer I was nine years old and did a yard sale to raise money for Rainbow Haven, a camp for under-privileged kids, volunteering has always been a big part of my life. It is a great way to meet people and give back to the community at the same time.

It's easy to find volunteer opportunities if you know where to look. It's something that's definitely embraced in the Muslim world. One of the Islamic religion's main pillars is charitable giving (or Zakat) where each year, Muslims are expected to donate a portion of their 'excess income' to those who are less fortunate. The support is more a monetary thing rather than a hands-on approach, which is where some of the systems are lacking in a country as young as the UAE. However, the movement is growing and there are several local charities that you can contact and many volunteer groups, usually run by expats, that have sprung up in support of various and assorted causes for which you can get involved.

The AWA has an active philanthropy committee, which I was involved in for two years as part of the scholarship committee, that also supports charities such as the Mission to Sea Farers (www.angelappeal.com), Al Ahsan Children's Centre (www.alahsan-org.ae) and the Dubai Centre for Special Needs (www.dcsneeds.ae). A whole slew of AWA members also volunteer on a regular basis at the USO (www.uso.org/dubai) when navy ships come in to port at Jebel Ali. It's a fun way to spend a few hours and the visiting sailors appreciate seeing the friendly faces.

Here are a few more charities that were recommended:

AdoptaCamp

- www.Facebook.com/AdoptaCamp
  Provides programs for men in 36 different labour camps plus a camp for abandoned men that provides food, water, gas, clothing and hope. Programs offered at the permanent camps that have been adopted include: English language classes (in association with the American University of Dubai); hygiene workshops; medical care; personal and emotional counselling; and care packages.

Dubai Cares

- www.dubaicares.ae
  Provides funding support for educational programs
  in developing countries focusing on four main areas:
  school infrastructure; school health and nutrition;
  water/sanitation and hygiene; and quality of
  education.

Gulf 4 Good

- www.gulf4good.org
  If you're looking for a trekking adventure/non-profit
  support combination, this is your charity. Adventure
  challenges are held year-round in various locations
  around the world and the funds raised go to a select
  charity in the area the challenge is held. Participants
  then have the chance to visit the charity as part of
  the trek.

Helping Hands UAE

- www.helpinghandsuae.com
  Started by British expats Roger and Elle Trow,
  Helping Hands provides support and supplies to
  needy workers and individuals living in the labour
  camps of the UAE.

K-9 and Feline Friends

- www.k9friends.com / www.felinefriendsdubai.com
  Both organisations foster stray and abandoned
  cats and dogs and try to find them new homes.
  Unbelievably, people move away and just dump
  their pets in the yard rather than bring them along.
  Shocking!

Room to Read

- www.roomtoread.org/dubai
  A charity that builds libraries and reading facilities
  for schools, provides scholarships for girls and
  publishes local language children's books in
  impoverished regions of the world.

The Dhaka Project

- www.thedhakaproject.org
  Started by an Emirates flight attendant after she
  saw the squalor of downtown Dhaka, the program
  provides short-term aid such as clothing, food,
  shelter and medical supplies as well as education
  and training to children and families in Dhaka,
  Bangladesh.

Volunteer in Dubai

- www.Facebook.com/Volunteerindubai
  Run by Lola Lopez, Volunteer in Dubai is an active,
  popular group that does volunteer work for both
  local and global charities. There's lots of roll up your
  sleeves, hands-on work to do and Lola's great at
  identifying needs and matching them to volunteers.

Sports

Personally, this would be last on my priority list as I don't
go for team sports. I'm more of a yoga girl (and there's
plenty of that too… I particularly liked Zen Yoga at Dubai
Media City, www.yoga.ae). However, I know for many
it's number one so here's a list of sports clubs that I've
come across or others have recommended.

Dubai Creek Striders Running Club

- www.dubaicreekstriders.com / www.dubaimarathon.org
  This club is usually working on training for the
  Dubai Marathon.

Dubai Hockey Club

- www.dubaihockeyclub.com
  It's actually field hockey… as a Canadian,
  I automatically assumed it was ice hockey.

Dubai Kitefly Club

- www.kitesurf.ae
  As in, on the water with your feet on a board and a kite pulling you through the waves. A kite surfing licence is required.

Dubai Offshore Sailing Club

- www.dosc.ae
  There is usually a waiting list for memberships so if you're a sailor, get your name on as soon as you arrive in Dubai. While you wait, there are always skippers looking for crew. Just check the bulletin board at the club.

Dubai Polo and Equestrian Club

- www.poloclubdubai.com
  You don't have to play. There's a social membership available and even if you're not a member it's a lot of fun just to go and watch the matches that are open to the public. Often the public matches are connected to a charity fundraiser.

Dubai Road Runners

- www.dubai-road-runners.com
  Welcomes runners of all ages and abilities and meets
  weekly at Safa Park. That's my favourite park in
  Dubai. Even though I'm not a runner, I love their
  motto, "You don't stop when you get old. You get
  old when you stop".

Dubai Roadsters Cycling Club

- www.dubairoadsters.com
  These guys are serious. I read that they have a
  practice night at the Dubai Motorway where you
  can 'come up to speed' with the rest before you join
  them on the road.

Dubai Rowing and Sculling Club

- www.dimc.ae
  Run by the Dubai International Marine Club, which
  also offers sailing and paddling lessons.

DuPlays

- http://dubai.duplays.com
  An organised sports league that's free to join.
  From cricket and football to table tennis and scuba
  diving, there's likely to be something on the list that
  grabs you.

EK Volleyball Club

- www.ekvolleyballclub.com
  Runs both beach volleyball and indoor volleyball at
  Dubai American Academy (during the summer).

Golf Clubs
- www.dubaigolf.info
  So many to choose from, too many to list. Here's
  a website to check out if you're a golfer. It gives a
  great overview of each course along with links to
  each course's own website.

Jebel Ali Shooting Club

- www.jebelali-international.com
  Part of Jebel Ali Golf Resort and Spa. The website
  address to get to the club is ridiculously long so
  use this link, click on the Jebel Ali Resort and Spa
  logo at the bottom and then go to the Sports and
  Leisure section.

Mina Seyahi Dubai Sailing Club

- www.dimc.ae
  Also run by the Dubai International Marine Club.

Sky Dive Dubai

- www.Skydivedubai.ae
  These guys are fun to watch from Barasti Bar (one of my favourite spots in Dubai) as they take off and parachute right next door. I prefer to keep my feet planted on terra firma but there are lunatics who like to push the envelope. If you're not qualified you can do a tandem jump with a professional.

Surf Dubai

- http://Surfingdubai.com
  A surfing club run by a guy who purportedly has a bachelor's degree in Surf Science and Technology. Who knew?

The Practicalities

You simply need the desire and equipment to play (sometimes clubs provide the equipment so desire is all that's needed).

The Five-Step Recap

Step 1

Get settled in and get all the formal connections made, job secured, house settled, phone and Internet connected and kids in school.

Step 2

Make a list of your favourite leisure (social, volunteer or sport) activities. You may want to do it in two columns: 'Just for Me' and 'For the Whole Family'.

Step 3

Review the list presented here, ask neighbours, colleagues and Internet forums to see if there are any groups that fulfil your leisure activity needs. Make a third column on your list and slot it in beside the related activity.

Step 4

Pick one to start with (I know you're tight for time but life-balance is critical).

Step 5

Join the group and go to a meeting, game, activity or event.

Tip

"So much Googling! I used <u>TimeOutDubai.com</u> and still do to find out what's happening in the city and to read restaurant reviews. I also got a lot of good info from <u>expatwoman.com</u>."

Amy from Canada

Case Study #1

"Research is what I do so I scoured the Internet for information about schools, places to live, churches, cultural differences, laws, and so on. My husband's company used *Intouch Relocation Services* (<u>www.intouchrelocations.com</u>) and they were helpful once we arrived in Dubai. By far, my most valuable resource was the other expats in Houston that I met who had lived in the region before. Their advice was invaluable to me."

Shirley W Ralston, MA/Christian Education, USA

Case Study #2

"Without a doubt, becoming involved in *Duplays* has really increased my ability to stay active and meet new people. *Duplays* is a social sports network that you can sign up for as an individual or a team. They offer sports of all kinds, some leagues offer different levels of sport too. I joined as soon as I moved here and have met many of my good friends because of it. I've played in their volleyball, softball and ultimate Frisbee leagues, not to mention their end of season social events that encompass four sports in one day. Highly recommended!"

Mary-Alison Lyman, Canadian

The Wrap Up

As you can see, the biggest challenge isn't finding the groups, it's actually combing through them all and selecting one to try. You can tailor-make a description of the perfect group for you and... voila! ... there it is. Some are better organised than others so be ready to try a few before you land on one that's just right. Or, you could be lucky and find your dream group on the first go around. Wouldn't that be awesome? And, don't be shy to go on your own. Every single person in the group will have been where you are at one point in time. You'll find loads of empathy and advice oozing from every corner. That's been my experience anyways.

Resources

Details of other useful books and references:

Books

"We were given *Dubai Explorer* as a gift before we came, and we did use it to research neighbourhoods, shopping, sights and restaurants," says Pam Rollings from Pittsburg, PA, USA who also has a blog, *Adventures in Dubailand.* "We didn't really use it until after we arrived in Dubai. Not that helpful except to give an overview.

"I actually made a few trips (four to be precise) over 12 months before making the final move," says Bijay Shah, national director, *BNI Middle East.* "Most of our research was based on word-of-mouth. A book I invested in was *Don't they know it's Friday* by Jeremy Williams."

Here are a few others to have a look at:

- *Burqalicious: The Dubai Diaries* by Becky Wicks

- *Career in Your Suitcase* by Jo Parfitt

- *Dubai & Co – Global Strategies for doing Business in Gulf States* by Aamir Rehman

- *Dubai Red Tape* – Explorer

- *Dubai The Journey* by Pranay Gupte

- *Dubai – The Vulnerability of Success* by Christopher Davidson

- *Expat Women Confessions: 50 Answers to your Real-Life Questions about Living Abroad* by Andrea Martin and Victoria Hepworth

- *Live, Work, Explore – Your Guide to Living in and Loving the Emirates* – Explorer

- *Living and Working in Dubai* by Pippa Sanderson

- *Living in Dubai* by Leslie Nicolas Nasr

- *Setting up in Dubai – Business Investors Guide* by Essam Tamimi

- *Should I Stay or Should I Go?* by Paul Allen

- *Success in the City: Dubai's Entrepreneurs Tell Their Story* by Kelly Lundberg

Magazines

- *Ahlan* – www.ahlan.ae

- *Aquarius* – http://gulfnews.com/about-gulf-news/al-nisr-portfolio/aquarius

- *Arabian Business* – www.arabianbusiness.com

- *Connector* – www.connector-dubai.com

- *Discover Dubai* – a *Connector* publication – www.connector-dubai.com/discover-dubai.html

- *Dubai Real Times* (official magazine of RERA) – http://emags.ae/magazines/drt

- *Emirates Home – Fresh Ideas for Modern Living* – www.emirateshome.com

- *Emirates Parent Plus* – www.emiratesparentplus.com

- *Emirates Woman* – www.motivate.ae

- *Friday Magazine* – a *Gulf News* publication – www.gulfnews.com

- *4Men* – http://gulfnews.com/about-gulf-news/al-nisr-portfolio/4men

- *FYI Dubai* – www.fyidubai.com

- *Masala* – www.masala.com

- *Middle East MICE & Events* – www.memicee.com

- *SME Advisor Middle East* – www.smeadvisor.me

- *Southeast Asia & UAE Home & Apartment Trends* – www.trendsideas.com

- *The Intelligent SME*, wwwtheintelligentsme.com

- *TimeOut Dubai* – www.timeoutdubai.com

- *UAE Digest* – http://emags.ae/magazines/ud

- *What's On* – www.motivate.ae

- You! And your life in the UAE – www.expatwoman.com/dubai/monthly_you_magazine.aspx

Newspapers

- *Emirates 24/7* – www.emirates247.com

- *Gulf News* – www.gulfnews.com

- *Khaleej Times* – www.khaleejtimes.com

- *7 Days* – www.7days.ae

- *The Gulf Today* – www.godubai.com/gulftoday

- *The National* – www.thenational.ae

- *Xpress* – www.xpress4me.com

Online News Aggregators

- *AME Info* – www.ameinfo.com

- *Zawya* – www.zawya.com

A recap of websites mentioned throughout the book

Accommodation

- *Al Marooj Rotana Hotel and Suites,* www.rotana.com

- *Al Nisr* Property Magazine, http://gulfnews.com/about-gulf-news/al-nisr-portfolio/property

- *Cheaper than Hotels*, www.cheaperthanhotels.ae

- *Crystal Living*, www.dubai.prostay.com/dubai_apartments/crystal_living_court

- *Easy Hotel*, www.easyhotel.com/hotels/dubai

- *ETA Star Hospitality*, www.etastarhospitality.com

- *Galleria Apartments*, www.thegalleria.hyatt.com

- *Gloria Hotel*, www.gloriahoteldubai.com

- *Golden Sands Hotel Apartments*, www.goldensandsduabi.com

- *Oasis Centre*, www.oasisbeachtower.com

- *Media Rotana*, www.rotana.com/rotanahotelandresorts/unitedarab emirates/dubai/mediarotana

- Property search and rent tracking, www.i-dar.net

- *Premier Inn,* www.global.premierinn.com

- *Radisson Blu*, www.radissonblu.com/hotel-dubaimarina

- *Room Bookings* (international), www.roombooking.com

- *Trade Centre Apartments*, www.dwtc.com

Banks

- *Abu Dhabi Commercial Bank*, www.adcb.com
- *Citibank*, www.citibank.com/uae
- *Commercial Bank of Dubai*, www.cbd.ae

- *Emirates NBD*, www.emiratesnbd.com

- *HSBC*, www.hsbc.ae

- *Lloyds TSB*, www.lloydstsb.ae

- *Mashraq Bank*, www.mashraqbank.com

- *Royal Bank of Scotland*, www.rbsbank.ae

Charities

- Adopt-a-Camp, www.Facebook.com/AdoptaCamp

- Al Ahsan Children's Centre, www.alahsan-org.ae

- Dubai Cares, www.dubaicares.ae

- Dubai Centre for Special Needs, www.dcsneeds.ae

- Feline Friends, www.felinefriends.com

- Gulf 4 Good, www.gulf4good.org

- Helping Hands UAE, www.helpinghandsuae.com

- K9 Friends, www.kpfriends.com

- Mission to Seafarers, www.angelappeal.com

- Room to Read, www.roomtoread.org/duabi

- The Dhaka Project, www.thedhakaproject.org

- USO Dubai, www.uso.org/dubai

- Volunteer in Dubai, www.facebook.com/volunteerindubai

Communities

- Dubai Marina, www.dubai-marina.com

- Emirates Hills, www.emirateshill.com

- Green Community, www.greencommunity.ae

- International City, www.internationalcity.ae

- Jumeirah Beach Residence, www.dubaipropertiesgroup.ae/en/properties/jumeirah-beach-residence

- Meadows and Springs, www.meadows-springs.com

- Old Town, www.theoldtown.ae

- Palm Jumeirah, www.palmjumeirah.ae

- Silicon Oasis, www.siliconoasis.org

Driving

- *Al Futtaim Motors*, www.alfuttaimmotors.ae

- *Auto Trader,* www.autotraderuae.com

- *Dubai FAQs*/Driving License Exemptions, www.dubaifaqs.com/driving-license-exchange-uae.php

- *Dubai Car Rental,* www.dubairentalcargroup.com

- *Emirates Driving Institute,* www.edi-uae.com

- *Insurance Index,* www.indexuae.com/top/business economy and economy/finance/insurance/3

- *International Car Shipping,* www.internationalcarshipping.net/shipping cars to dubai.html

- *Kelly Bluebook,* www.kbb.com/whats-my-car-worth

- *Roadside Assistance,* www.aaaemirates.com or www.rac.ae

- *Salik,* www.salik.ae

Entertainment

- *Emirates Festival of Literature*, www.eaifl.com

- *Grand Cinemas*, www.grandcinemas.com

- *Madinat Theatre*, www.madinattheatre.com

- *Ski Dubai,* www.skidxb.com

- *TimeOut Dubai*-Kids, www.timeoutdubai.com/kids

- *TimeOut*-Tickets, www.timeouttickets.com

- *Wild Wadi*, www.jumeirah.com/hotels-and-resorts/wildwadi

Government

- Department of Naturalization, www.dnrd.ae

- DEWA (Dubai Electricity and Water Authority), www.dewa.gov.ae/default.aspx

- DEWA Consumer Guide, www.dewa.gov.ae/consumers/consumerguide/default.aspx

- DEWA Application, http://e-services.dewa.gov.ae/activation/activationrequest.aspx

- Dubai Health Authority, www.dohms.gov.ae

- Dubai Police, www.dubaipolice.gov.ae

- Dubai Real Estate Regulatory Agency (RERA), www.rpdubai.ae

- Emirates Identity Authority, www.emiratesid.ae

- Free Zones, www.uaefreezones.com

- Ministry of Health, www.moh.gov.ae

- Typing Centres, www.emiratesid.ae/en/process-and-fees/registration-   plan.aspx

- UAE Ministry of Environment and Water Animal Health, www.moew.gov.ae

Healthcare

- *800-Doctor*, www.800doctor.com

- *Doctor Dubai*, www.doctor-dubai.com

- *Silla*, www.silla.ae

Maid Services

- *Dial-a-Maid*, http://duabimaids.ae

- *Focus Cleaning*, www.focusmaids.com/contactus.html

- *Home Maids*, www.homemaids.ae

- *Howdra*, www.howdra.ae

- *Molly Maid*, www.mollymaid.com

- *Ready Maids*, www.readymaidsdubai.com

- *Right Maids*, www.rightmaids.net

- *Solutions Hygiene*, www.solutionshygiene.com

Networking (Professional/Social/Sports)

- *Allo Expat*, www.alloexpat.com/dubai_expat_forum

- American Business Council of Dubai and the Northern Emirates, www.abcdubai.com

- American Business Group, www.americanbusinessgroup.org

- American Women's Association, www.awadubai.org

- ANZA – (Australians and New Zealanders), www.anzauae.org

- Arab Business Club, www.arabbusinessclub.com

- British Business Group, www.britbiz-uae.com

- Business Networking International (BNI), www.bni.com

- Canadian Business Council, www.cbc-dubai.com

- Danes in Dubai, www.danesindubai.com

- Desert Speak, www.desertspeak.com

- Dubai Caledonian Society, www.dubaicaledoniansociety.com

- Dubai Chamber of Commerce and Industry, www.dubaichamber.com

- Dubai Community Theatre and Arts Centre (DUCTAC), www.ductac.org

- Dubai Creek Striders Running Club, www.dubaicreekstriders.com

- Dubai Dads' Club, www.dubaidadsclub.com

- Dubai Forums, www.dubaiforums.com

- Dubai Hockey Club, www.dubaihockeyclub.com

- Dubai Irish Society, www.irishindubai.com

- Dubai Kitefly Club, www.kitesurf.ae

- Dubai Ladies Club, www.dubailadiesclub.com

- Dubai Natural History Group, www.enhg.org/dubai/dubai.htm

- Dubai Offshore Sailing Club, www.dosc.ae

- Dubai Polo and Equestrian Club, www.poloclubdubai.com

- Dubai Road Runners, www.dubai-road-runners.com

- Dubai Roadsters Cycling Club, www.dubairoadsters.com

- Dubai Rowing and Sculling Club, www.dimc.ae

- DuPlays, http://dubai.duplays.com

- EK Volleyball Club, www.ekvolleyballclub.com

- Emirates Mac, www.emiratesmac.com

- *Expat Woman*, www.expatwoman.com

- *Expat Women*, www.expatwomen.com

- *Expat Echo*, www.expatecho.com

- Golf Clubs, www.dubaigolf.info

- *Heels & Deals*, www.heelsanddeals.org

- International Business Women's Group (IBWG), www.ibwgdubai.com

- InterNations, www.internations.org/dubai-expats

- Irish Business Network Dubai, www.irishsocietydubai.com

- Jebel Ali Shooting Club, www.jebelali-international.com

- *LinkedIn*, www.linkedin.com

- *Meetup Dubai*, www.meetup.com/cities/ae/dubai

- Mina Seyahi Dubai Sailing Club, www.dimc.ae

- SolidariTea Arabia, www.facebook.com/Solidaritea

- Sky Dive Dubai, www.Skydivedubai.ae

- Surf Dubai, http://Surfingdubai.com

- TEDx Dubai, www.tedxdubai.com

- Toast Masters Dubai Chapter,
  www.dubaitoastmasters.org

Online Shopping

- *Aido*, www.aido.com

- *Alship*, www.alship.com

- *Amazon*, www.amazon.com

- *Arabian Offer*, www.arabianoffer.com

- *Burjmall*, www.burjmall.com

- *Carrefour Online Shopping*, www.ic4uae.com

- *Cobone*, www.cobone.com

- *Emirates Avenue*, www.emiratesavenue.com

- *Expedia,* www.expedia.com

- *Flowers UAE,* www.flowers.ae

- *Food on Click,* www.foodonclick.com

- *Go Nabit,* www.gonabit.com

- *Groupon,* www.groupon.com

- *Mycroburst,* www.mycroburst.com

- *Nahel,* www.nahel.com

- *QuickDubai,* www.quickdubai.com

- *Shop and Ship,* www.shopandship.com

- *Souq,* www.souq.com

- *Sukar,* www.sukar.com

- *Spend Wisor,* www.spendwisor.com

- *Try Ask Sunday,* www.tryasksunday.com

- *Yalla Banana,* www.yallabanana.com

Realtors/Relocation Companies

- *Allsopp and Allsopp*, www.allsoppandallsopp.com

- *Better Homes*, www.bhomes.com

- *Executive Expatriate Relocations*, http://dubaimoving.com

- *In Touch Relocations*, www.intouchrelocations.com

- *Move One, Inc.*, www.moveoneinc.com

- *Property Finder*, www.propertyfinder.ae

Schools/Education

- American School of Dubai, www.asdubai.org

- Dubai American Academy, www. gemsaa-dubai.com

- Dubai British School, www.dubaibritishschool.ae

- Dubai College, www.dubaicollege.org

- French Lycee Pompidou, www.lfigp.org

- GEMS Jumeirah Primary School,
  www.jumeirahprimaryschool.com

- GEMS Wellington International School,
  www.wellingtoninternationalschool.com

- GEMS Wellington Primary School, www.gemswps.com

- Horizon Primary, www.horizonschooldubai.com

- International Baccalaureate Curriculum, www.ibo.org

- Jebel Ali Primary School, www.jebelalischool.org

- Jumeirah College, www.gemsjc.com

- Jumeirah English Speaking School, www.jess.sch.ae

- Kings Dubai School, www.kingsdubai.com

- Oasis Children's Nursery,
  www.childrensoasisnursery.com

- Repton, www.reptondubai.org

- Star International, http://starschoolmirdif.com

Services

- *du*, www.du.ae

- *du Hotspots*, www.du.ae/en/wifilocations

- *Emirates Gas*, www.emiratesgas.ae

- *Emirates Post*, www.emiratespostuae.com

- *Emirates Post locations*,
  www.dubaifaqs.com/post-offices-dubai.php

- *Etisalat*, www.etisalat.ae

- *Etisalat Hotspots*,
  www.etisalat.ae/assets/file/hotspots/userguide/index.html

- *MagicJack*, www.magicjack.com

- *Web Phone*, www.webphone.com

Other

- *Big 5 Personality Test*, www.outofservice.com/bigfive

- *Blogger*, www.blogspot.com

- *Carrefour*, www.carrefouruae.com

- *Dubai City Information*, www.dubaicityinfo.com

- *Dubai FAQs/Visa Information*,
  www.dubaifaqs.com/visa-dubai.php

- *Dubai International Financial Centre*, www.difc.ae

- *Dubai Kennel and Cattery*, www.dkc.ae

- *Elance*, www.elance.com

- *Entrepreneur*, www.entrepreneur.com

- *Expat Forum*, www.expatforum.com

- *Expatica*, www.expatica.com

- *Guide to Dubai*, www.guidetodubai.com

- *I was an Expat Wife,* www.iwasanexpatwife.com

- *Jumeirah Mosque,*
  www.cultures.ae/jumeirah_mosque_visit.php

- *Marhaba*, www.marhabaservices.com

- *Monster Gulf*, www.monstergulf.com

- *Naukri*, www.naukri.com

- *oDesk,* www.odesk.com

- *Twitter,* www.twitter.com

- *WordPress,* www.wordpress.com

About the Author

@*Home in Dubai* author, Anne O'Connell, has been an expat since 1993 when she and her husband escaped the cold of Toronto, Canada and moved to Fort Lauderdale, Florida. They enjoyed the sun and sand for 14 years, while she worked in the PR field, and then decided it was time for a new adventure. Heading for even more sun and sand, they moved to Dubai in late 2007.

After getting settled, O'Connell started a freelance copy writing business specialising in marketing, corporate communications, public relations, social media and website content. Along with being a writer and editor for the @*Home in...* series, O'Connell is also a contributing writer for *Suite101* and has been recognized twice with an Editor's Choice Award on the *Fiction Writers' Platform*.

From Spanish emersion in Guatemala to swimming with the elephants in Koh Chang, Thailand, O'Connell's adventurous spirit has taken her all over the world. She has visited 25 countries with many more to explore. Moving to Dubai gave her the opportunity to see a whole new part of the world, to experience new cultures and allow her to focus on her true passion – writing.

O'Connell grew up in Halifax, Nova Scotia and has a bachelor of public relations from Mount St. Vincent University.

Acknowledgements

I'm happy to say that I have been inspired and mentored by my publisher at Summertime publishing, Jo Parfitt. The first time I met her was actually via Skype when she joined my authors group to give us some tips. She was so helpful and enthusiastic about all our projects that she offered to come to Dubai to conduct a workshop on how to get your book written and published. After her second trip to Dubai for another workshop, we were well on our way to working together on this project.

A special thanks also to Jeanette Todd, who donated her time as my legal consultant and research assistant. She constantly sent great website links and interesting people to fill in the *@Home in Dubai* survey. Heartfelt thanks also goes to my good friend (who I actually knew when I lived in Florida), blogger and freelance writer, Katie Foster, my fellow Dubai explorer, navigator, sounding board and contributor. Thanks to Katie and Linda Hoagland who both proofread and edited the manuscript before I sent it to Jo.

Special thanks to my Flamingo Authors group. Everyone was always just an email or phone call away when I had a research gap to fill (especially Katie, Amy, Debbie and Susan C, but just about everyone did the survey).

And to all the survey respondents! Thanks for sharing your stories and advice.

Finally, a big, heartfelt thanks to my husband, Doug, for supporting my writing habit. He doesn't mind that I hermit myself away for hours on end, as long as I come out smiling... which I inevitably do, because I'm doing something I love.

Happy Trails to everyone!

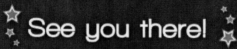

Also Published by **summertimepublishing**

"Everything you need for a career on the move"

a **career** in your **suitcase**

THIRD EDITION

completely revised & updated

Jo Parfitt

with Galen Tinder, Huw Francis, Carl Machdoe and Mary Van Der Boon

SUNSHINE
SOUP

NOURISHING THE GLOBAL SOUL

Jo Parfitt

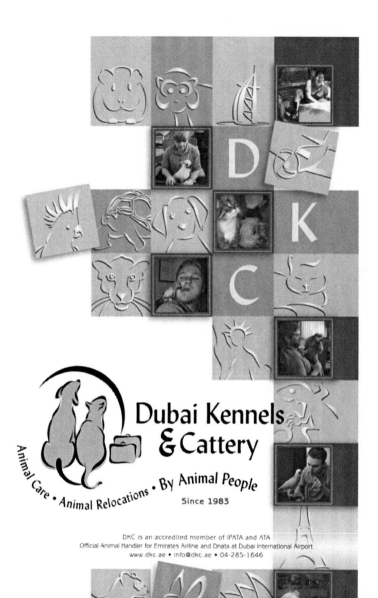

Dubai Kennels & Cattery

Animal Care • Animal Relocations • By Animal People

Since 1983

DKC is an accredited member of IPATA and ATA
Official Animal Handler for Emirates Airline and Dnata at Dubai International Airport
www.dkc.ae • info@dkc.ae • 04-285-1646